A CALL TO ACTION

Women, Religion, Violence, and Power

JIMMY CARTER

Simon & Schuster

New York   London   Toronto   Sydney   New Delhi

SIMON & SCHUSTER
1230 Avenue of the Americas
New York, NY 10020

First Simon & Schuster hardcover edition March 2014

SIMON & SCHUSTER and colophon are registered trademarks
of Simon & Schuster, Inc.

For information about special discounts for bulk purchases, please
contact Simon & Schuster Special Sales at 1-866-506-1949 or
business@simonandschuster.com.

The Simon & Schuster Speakers Bureau can bring authors to your
live event. For more information or to book an event, contact
the Simon & Schuster Speakers Bureau at 1-866-248-3049 or visit
our website at www.simonspeakers.com.

Interior design by Claudia Martinez
Jacket design by Christopher Lin

Manufactured in the United States of America

10 9 8 7 6 5 4 3 2 1

Library of Congress Cataloging-in-Publication Data is available.

ISBN 978-1-4767-7395-7
ISBN 978-1-4767-7397-1 (ebook)

To Karin Ryan,

and the countless women and girls
whose abuse and deprivation she strives to alleviate

CONTENTS

CONTENTS | viii

A CALL TO ACTION

INTRODUCTION

All the elements in this book concerning prejudice, discrimination, war, violence, distorted interpretations of religious texts, physical and mental abuse, poverty, and disease fall disproportionately on women and girls.

I saw the ravages of racial prejudice as I grew up in the Deep South, when for a century the U.S. Supreme Court and all other political and social authorities accepted the premise that black people were, in some basic ways, inferior to white people. Even those in the dominant class who disagreed with this presumption remained relatively quiet and enjoyed the benefits of the prevailing system. Carefully selected Holy Scriptures were quoted to justify this discrimination in the name of God.

There is a similar system of discrimination, extending far beyond a small geographical region to the entire globe; it touches every nation, perpetuating and expanding the trafficking in human slaves, body mutilation, and even legitimized murder on a massive scale. This system is based on the presumption that men and boys are superior to women and girls, and it is supported by some male religious leaders who distort the Holy Bible, the Koran, and other sacred texts to perpetuate their claim that females are, in some basic ways, inferior to them, unqualified to serve God on equal terms. Many men disagree but remain quiet in order to enjoy the benefits of their dominant status. This false premise provides a justification for sexual discrimination in almost every realm of secular and religious life. Some men even cite this premise to justify physical punishment of women and girls.

Another factor contributing to the abuse of women and girls is an acceptance of violence, from unwarranted armed combat to excessive and biased punishment for those who violate the law. In too many cases, we use violence as a first rather than a last resort, so that even deadly violence has become commonplace.

My own experiences and the testimony of courageous women from all regions and all major religions have made it clear to me that as a result of these two factors there is a pervasive denial of equal rights to women, more than half of all human beings, and this discrimination results in tangible harm to all of us, male and female.

My wife, Rosalynn, and I have visited about 145 countries, and the nonprofit organization we founded, The Carter Center, has had active projects in more than half of them. We have had opportunities in recent years to interact directly among the people, often in remote villages in the jungles and deserts. We have learned a lot about their personal affairs, particularly that financial inequality has been growing more rapidly with each passing decade. This is true both between rich and poor countries and among citizens within them. In fact, the disparity in net worth and income in the United States has greatly increased since my time in the White House. By 2007 the income of the middle 60 percent of Americans had increased at a rate twice as high as that of the bottom 20 percent. And the rate of increase for the top 1 percent was over fifteen times higher, primarily because of the undue influence of wealthy people who invest in elections and later buy greater benefits for themselves in Washington and in state capitals. As the conservative columnist George Will writes, "Big government *inevitably* drives an upward distribution of wealth to those whose wealth, confidence and sophistication enable them to manipulate government."

Yet although economic disparity is a great and growing problem, I have become convinced that *the most serious and unaddressed worldwide challenge is the deprivation and abuse of women and girls*, largely caused by a false interpretation of carefully selected religious texts and a growing tolerance of violence and warfare, unfortunately following the example set during my lifetime by the United States. In addition to the unconscionable human suffering, almost embarrassing to acknowledge, there is a devastating effect on economic prosperity caused by the loss of contributions of at least half the human beings on earth. This is not just a women's issue. It is not confined to the poorest countries. It affects us all.

After focusing for a few years on the problem of gender discrimination through our human rights program at The Carter Center, I began to speak out more forcefully about it. Because of this, I was asked to address the Parliament of the World's Religions, an audience of several thousand assembled in Australia in December 2009, about the vital role of religion in providing a foundation for countering the global scourge of gender abuse. My remarks represented the personal views of a Christian layman, a Bible teacher for more than seventy years, a former political leader.

I reminded the audience that in dealing with each other, we are guided by international agreements as well as our own moral values, most often derived from the Universal Declaration of Human Rights, the Bible, the Koran, and other cherished texts that proclaim a commitment to justice and mercy, equality of treatment between men and women, and a duty to alleviate suffering. However, some selected scriptures are interpreted, almost exclusively by powerful male leaders within the Christian, Jewish, Muslim, Hindu, Buddhist, and other faiths, to proclaim the lower status of women and girls. This claim that women are inferior before God spreads to the secular world to justify gross and sustained acts of discrimination and violence against them. This includes unpunished rape and other sexual abuse, infanticide of newborn girls and abortion of female fetuses, a worldwide trafficking in women and girls, and so-called honor killings of innocent women who are raped, as well as the less violent but harmful practices of lower pay and fewer promotions for women and greater political advantages for men. I mentioned some notable achievements of women despite these handicaps and described struggles within my own religious faith. I called on believers, whether Protestant, Catholic, Coptic, Jew, Muslim, Buddhist, Hindu, or tribal, to study these violations of our basic moral values and to take corrective action.

No matter what our faith may be, it is impossible to imagine a God who is unjust.

ZAINAH ANWAR,
FOUNDER OF SISTERS IN ISLAM, MALAYSIA

In the following pages I will outline how I learned more and more about these issues, as a child, a submarine officer, a farmer, and a church leader during the civil rights struggle, as a governor and a president, as a college professor, and in the global work of The Carter Center. During the nine decades of my life I have become increasingly aware of and concerned about the immense number of and largely ignored gender-based crimes. There are reasons for hope that some of these abuses can be ended when they become better known and understood. I hope that this book will help to expose these violations to a broader audience and marshal a more concerted effort to address this profound problem.

I will explore the links between religion-based assertions of male dominance over women, as well as the ways that our "culture of violence" contributes to the denial of women's rights. I maintain that male dominance over women is a form of oppression that often leads to violence. We cannot make progress in advancing women's rights if we do not examine these two underlying factors that contribute to the abuse of women.

In August 2013 I joined civil rights leaders and two other American presidents at the Lincoln Memorial to commemorate the fiftieth anniversary of Martin Luther King Jr.'s "I Have a Dream" speech, delivered there in 1963. As I looked out on the crowd and thought about the book I was writing, my thoughts turned to a different speech that King made, in New York City four years later, about America's war in Vietnam, in which my oldest son was serving. King asserted, "I knew that I could never again raise my voice against the violence of the oppressed in the ghettos without having first spoken clearly to the greatest purveyor of violence in the world today—my own government." King went on to ask that we Americans broaden our view to look at human freedom as inextricably linked with our commitment to peace and nonviolence.

Using this same logic, it is not possible to address the rights of women, the human and civil rights struggle of our time, without looking at factors that encourage the acceptance of violence in our society—violence that inevitably affects women disproportionately. The problem is not only militarism in foreign policy but also the resort to lethal violence and excessive deprivation of freedom in our criminal justice system when rehabilitation alternatives could be pursued. Clearly, short-term political advantages that come with being "tough on criminals" or "tough on terrorism" do not offer solutions to issues like persistent crime, sexual violence, and global terrorism.

I realize that violence is not more prevalent today than in previous periods of human history, but there is a difference. We have seen visionary standards adopted by the global community that espouse peace and human rights, and the globalization of information ensures that the violation of these principles of nonviolence by a powerful and admired democracy tends to resonate throughout the world community. We should have advanced much further in the realization of women's rights, given these international commitments to peace and the rule of law. Instead many of the gains made in advancing human rights since World War II are placed at risk by reliance on injury to others as a means to solve our problems.

We must not forget that there is always an underlying basis of moral and religious principles involved. In August 2013 Pope Francis stated quite simply that in addition to the idea that violence does not bring real solutions to societal problems, its use is contrary to the will of God: "Faith and violence are incompatible." This powerful statement exalting peace and compassion is one on which all faiths can agree.

In June 2013 The Carter Center brought together religious leaders, scholars, and activists who are working to align religious life with the advancement of girls' and women's full equality. We called this a Human Rights Defenders Forum. Throughout this book I have inserted brief statements from some of these defenders that offer a rich array of ideas and perspectives on the subject.

1 | MY CHILDHOOD

I grew up west of Plains, Georgia, in the relatively isolated rural community of Archery, where about fifty African American and two white families lived, ours and that of the foreman of a repair crew for the Seaboard Airline Railroad. Then and even now there is a spirit of chivalry in the South, and I was taught to respect all women. My mother, a registered nurse, was often away from home at all hours, especially when she was on private duty, serving in her patient's home for twenty hours a day. She would come home at 10 o'clock at night, bathe, wash her uniform, leave a written list of chores and instructions for me and my sisters, and return to her patient at 2 A.M. When this was her schedule, my parents hired one or two black women to prepare meals for us and care for the house. Even in those times of racial segregation, my father ordained that we treat these women with deference and obedience, and I never knew of a time when they failed to deserve this high regard.

I stayed in the house as little as possible, preferring to be with my father working in the fields or the woods, at the barn or blacksmith shop, or with my friends on the creek and in the forest when there was no work to be done. I was immersed in an African American culture, with my black playmates and fellow field workers.

My heroine was Rachel Clark, whose husband, Jack, cared for my family's livestock and farm equipment and who rang the farm bell an hour before daylight to rouse everyone for the day's work. In *Always a Reckoning*, my first and longest poem is "Rachel." I describe her as having "an aura like a queen" and never being called on by white people for menial personal service such as cooking, washing clothes, or doing housework. She and I were bonded in many ways, as she taught me how to fish, how to recognize trees, birds, and flowers, and how I should relate to God and to other people. Rachel was famous for picking more cotton and shaking and stacking more peanuts than anyone else, man or woman. There was a quiet but intense contest in the field each day at harvest time when pay was based on accomplishment, and she was always the best. This was a source of great prestige in our agricultural community. I would work beside her as she picked two rows of cotton to my one and sometimes helped me stay even with her as we moved back and forth across the field. I relished the nights I spent with Rachel and Jack, sleeping on a pallet on their floor. I was not aware of distinctions among people based on race or sex in those early and innocent days of my life.

My basic attitude toward women was not changed when I was only six years old and acquired my first knowledge of adult sexual and racial relationships on my daily visits to the nearby town of Plains. The peanut crop on our farm matured during summer vacations from school, and my father permitted me to go into the field, pull up a small wagonload of peanut plants by their roots, and haul them to our yard. There I plucked about ten pounds of the mature pods from the vines, drew a bucket of water from the well, carefully washed away the clinging dirt, and kept the green pods overnight in a pot of salty water. Early the next morning I boiled the peanuts, divided them into twenty small paper bags, and then toted them in a basket down the railroad track about two miles to Plains, where I sold them for a nickel a package.

I would arrive there early every morning for weeks, except Sundays, and go in and out of the grocery stores, blacksmith shops, stables, gas stations, the post office, and farm warehouses until my basket was empty. The traveling salesmen and other men ignored me as though I were a piece of furniture, and would gossip, tell dirty jokes, and give lurid accounts of their sexual exploits as though I were not there. Having been taught to respect my mother and all other women, I was surprised to learn which wives around the town were said to be unfaithful, which girls were "putting out," how often the men went to the whorehouses in the nearby city of Albany, and how much it cost. What surprised me most was that many of these white men preferred black women, when other interracial social contact was completely taboo. These were things I never discussed with either of my parents.

I began to realize for the first time that I lived in a community where our Bible lessons were interpreted to accommodate the customs and ethical standards that were most convenient. There was no such thing as divorce because we lived by the admonition in Mark 10:7–9, "For this reason a man will leave his father and mother and be united to his wife, and the two will become one flesh. So they are no longer two, but one. Therefore what God has joined together let man not put asunder." It was well known, however, that some men were living with unmarried women and some with the wives of other men. My godmother, the head nurse at the hospital, was married to one man but lived with another, a senior medical doctor in town; they had a baby who was named after me. Two farmers who lived near each other swapped their entire families, wives and children, and so far as I know lived happily ever after without worrying about such details as marriage licenses.

I was caught up in an even more generic misinterpretation of the Holy Scriptures concerning racial inequality, which has affected my entire life. I came to realize that rationalization is a human trait, of which we are all guilty at times. I certainly do not like to admit that any of my deeply held beliefs are in error, and when any are challenged I seek every source of evidence to prove that I am right. The ultimate source of authenticity for my fellow religious believers was the Holy Bible, which provided the foundation for our Christian faith. The Hebrew text of the Bible, the New Testament, and the Koran, plus ancient interpretations, are complex combinations of history, biography, and the teachings and actions of those we revere. Many devout people consider these texts to be inerrant—incapable of containing error—despite the fact that some verses directly contradict others in the same holy book, and some ancient statements, such as descriptions of stars falling from the sky to the earth, are contrary to scientific knowledge. The overall messages or themes of the scriptures can be discerned, however, and they almost invariably espouse the moral and ethical values of peace, justice, compassion, forgiveness, and care for the destitute and those in need.

We can forget or ignore these principles if their violation is to our social, economic, or political benefit. I experienced this for almost three decades of my life, when I was part of an American society that espoused the "separate but equal" ruling of the U.S. Supreme Court. Although it was apparent to everyone that the practical application emphasized *separate* rather than *equal*, the legal system of racial segregation prevailed until the civil rights laws were adopted in the mid-1960s.

The segregation laws were observed throughout Georgia, the rest of the Deep South, and to some degree in all other states, and in my early years I never knew them to be questioned. It is difficult now for me to believe that no serious objections were raised when my only friends and playmates and their families went to a different church than ours, attended inferior schools, and could not vote or serve on a jury. When one of my black friends and I went to a movie in the county seat we rode in separate cars on the passenger train and sat at separate levels in the theater. These were practices in which I was complicit. Distinguished religious leaders visited our Plains Baptist Church on occasion to preach sermons based on selected scriptures about how it was God's will that the races be separated, and they even mentioned with pride how far we had progressed since slavery had ended in the United States—although forced servitude was obviously condoned by the biblical texts they quoted.

I have a hazy memory of the first time I was conscious of segregation in my own life, when I was about fourteen, and later I wrote a poem about it called "The Pasture Gate." I was returning with two friends from working in the field, and when we got to the gate between our barn lot and the pasture they stood back to let me go through first. I thought there might be a wire to trip me—we frequently played such pranks on each other—but later I surmised that their parents had told them that, as we were now older, we were no longer to treat each other as equals.

Not yet seriously questioned or rejected by many secular and religious leaders is a parallel dependence on selected verses of scripture to justify a belief that, even or especially in the eyes of God, women and girls are inferior to their husbands and brothers.

If women are equal in the eyes of God, why are we not equal in the eyes of men?

ZAINAH ANWAR,

FOUNDER OF SISTERS IN ISLAM, MALAYSIA

There has long been a distinction in societal attitudes toward men and women who engage in extramarital sex. In the summer 2013 issue of *Christian Ethics Today* is an article by a young Canadian woman who, at nineteen, was a devout unmarried Christian, stigmatized by her pastor when he learned she had participated in a sexual act. Before an assembly of young people, this spiritual leader decided to teach her a lesson by analogy; he passed around a glass of water and had each person spit in it, then asked, "Now who wants to drink this?" Now happily married and with three children, her declaration that she is not "damaged goods" and unworthy of a decent husband is intended to reassure the four out of five evangelical Christian women who have had sex before marriage that they are acceptable in the eyes of God and should not be defamed.

I read her statement with some discomfort, but with a realization that it was both true and helpful. My hometown was and still is deeply religious. We have eleven churches to serve a total population of fewer than eight hundred, and they are still the centers of our social life. When I was a teenager it was rare for boys and girls to sleep together unless it was assumed by them and their families that they were soon to be married. There were just two or three girls who were known to be willing to depart from these standards, but it was considered normal among boys to take advantage of any sexual opportunity. Rosalynn and I were deeply in love, and we decided to wait until after our wedding to consummate our marriage. It would have been completely out of character for her to do otherwise, but I was always reluctant to let other young men know that I was a virgin, feeling that it was somehow a reflection on my manhood.

I have come to realize that societal standards—at least in the Western world—are much different from what I knew as a youth, but there is still a sharp difference between those that apply to boys and those that apply to girls. I still believe that abstinence is the best choice for both, but condemnation and disgrace are not appropriate, and there should not be any distinctions in rules of behavior for males and females.

2 | COMMITMENT TO PEACE AND WOMEN'S RIGHTS

I was serving as an officer in the U.S. Navy during the latter days of World War II and the first years of peace and was fascinated, even then, with political affairs. I followed closely the formation of the United Nations and kept a copy of its Charter and by-laws on the ship with me. There was a consensus among political leaders and the general public of all nations that the time had come for an end to devastating wars and a common commitment to seek peaceful alternatives to inevitable disputes. The dominant players and permanent members of the United Nations Security Council were the five major nations that had been victorious and were determined to establish insurmountable impediments to armed conflict and to ensure that Germany, Japan, and Italy, the defeated aggressors, would be pacified. The stated purpose of the United Nations was "to promote cooperation in security, economic development, social progress, human rights, civil liberties, political freedom, democracy, and lasting world peace." Leaders also considered it imperative to take common action to prevent a repetition of horrible human rights crimes, most notably the Holocaust and the deaths of millions of others who could not escape the consequences of ethnic or racial hatred.

During those halcyon days these same leaders moved to provide a permanent international foundation of justice and equality for all people. The United Nations Charter committed all member states to promote "universal respect for, and observance of, human rights and fundamental freedoms for all without distinction as to race, sex, language, or religion." The next step was more specific, and, with special leadership in the American delegation from former first lady Eleanor Roosevelt, the organization produced the thirty simple and clear articles that fulfilled the bold and challenging expectations of the Charter.

The Universal Declaration of Human Rights was ratified in 1948 by a vote of 48 to 0. There were eight abstentions, including from the Soviet bloc, which objected to the right of citizens (especially Jews) to emigrate from their home country, and South Africa, whose all-white apartheid government did not consider black people deserving of equal status. It is significant that there were no objections raised to the guarantee of equal rights for women and girls, except that Saudi Arabia, which also abstained, opposed the provision guaranteeing equality within marriage. Eight Islamic governments voted in favor of the Declaration. There is no possibility that these same commitments could be made today, as memories of the devastation of world war have faded, the five permanent members are often at odds and no longer as dominant, and there is more polarization within regions and individual countries.

It is helpful to examine the document in some detail to understand the universal commitment to equal status between men and women in all walks of life. The full text can be found on the Internet. Every word applies to women as well as men, but I have excerpted and emphasized phrases that apply directly to the subject of this book. Some of them are surprising in their specificity and relevance now.

> PREAMBLE. Whereas recognition of the inherent dignity and of the equal and inalienable rights *of all members of the human family* is the foundation of freedom, justice and peace in the world, . . .

Whereas the peoples of the United Nations have in the Charter reaffirmed their faith in fundamental human rights, in the dignity and worth of the human person *and in the equal rights of men and women* and have determined to promote social progress and better standards of life in larger freedom . . .

Article 1. *All human beings* are born free and equal in dignity and rights.

Article 2. Everyone is entitled to all the rights and freedoms set forth in this Declaration, *without distinction of any kind*, such as race, color, *sex*, language, religion, political or other opinion, national or social origin, property, birth or other status.

Article 4. No one shall be held in slavery or servitude; slavery and the slave trade shall be prohibited in all their forms.

Article 5. No one shall be subjected to torture or to cruel, inhuman or degrading treatment or punishment.

Article 16. (1) Men and women *of full age*, without any limitation due to race, nationality or religion, have the right to marry and to found a family. They are entitled to *equal rights as to marriage, during marriage and at its dissolution.*

(2) *Marriage shall be entered into only with the free and full consent of the intending spouses.*

Article 21. (3) The will of the people shall be the basis of the authority of government; this shall be expressed in periodic and genuine elections which shall be by *universal and equal suffrage* and shall be held by secret vote or by equivalent free voting procedures.

Article 23. (2) Everyone, without any discrimination, has the right to *equal pay for equal work.*

Article 25. (2) *Motherhood and childhood are entitled to special care and assistance.* All children, whether born in or out of wedlock, shall enjoy the same social protection.

Article 26. (1) Everyone has the *right to education*.
(3) Parents have a prior right to choose the kind of education
that shall be given to their children.

These were clear and unequivocal commitments made by the world's
leaders to be binding in perpetuity. It is shameful that these solemn international agreements, later ratified by national legislative bodies, are
being violated so blatantly. Some people may even find them outdated
and naïve. It must be presumed that even the authors of the Declaration realized at the time that many of the world's religious leaders,
who remained remarkably silent, did then and always would exempt
themselves and their compliant followers from the granting of these
guaranteed equal rights to women and girls.

War and violence against women not only have similar social, cultural, and religious supports, they are mutually reinforcing. These supports allow societies to tolerate conditions
in which a third of women and girls can be treated violently,
without mass outcry and rebellion. When we challenge the
attitudes and norms that enable violence against women, we
also are helping to confront the conditions that support war.

REV. DR. SUSAN BROOKS THISTLETHWAITE,

PROFESSOR OF THEOLOGY AND FORMER PRESIDENT,

CHICAGO THEOLOGICAL SEMINARY

It is a tragedy that this declaration of guaranteed equal rights for
all people has not been realized and that there has also been a general and growing acceptance of warfare and violence instead of peace.
The concept of the United Nations Security Council as the primary
arbiter of disputes and of individual nations resorting to armed combat only as a last resort and to protect themselves has been subverted

by divisions among the five permanent members, each of whom has strong regional alliances and interests and a veto over any final decision.

More than any other nation, the United States has been almost constantly involved in armed conflict and, through military alliances, has used war as a means of resolving international and local disputes. Since the birth of the United Nations, we have seen American forces involved in combat in Afghanistan, Bosnia, Cambodia, the Dominican Republic, El Salvador, Greece, Grenada, Haiti, Iraq, Korea, Kosovo, Kuwait, Laos, Lebanon, Libya, Nicaragua, Panama, Serbia, Somalia, and Vietnam, and more recently with lethal attacks in Pakistan, Somalia, Yemen, and other sovereign nations. There were no "boots on the ground" in some of these countries; instead we have used high-altitude bombers or remote-control drones. In these cases we rarely acknowledge the tremendous loss of life and prolonged suffering among people in the combat zones, even after our involvement in the conflict is ended.

Some of these military actions may have been justified in the defense of our nation or its vital interests, but the tragedy is that their easy adoption, sometimes without the consent or knowledge of the public or most members of Congress, has made the resort to violence a natural and even popular facet of foreign policy. Some devout Christians have been in the forefront of advocating warfare even when the choice was hotly debated among the general public. "An eye for an eye" has become more important to them than the teachings of Jesus as the Prince of Peace.

When America is questioned about its military involvement throughout the world, the increasingly natural and common answer is, "We need to show our strength and resolve and to take military action when necessary to achieve our goals." Without debating the political need, peaceful alternatives, or the ultimate success or failure of these military adventures, the previously firm commitment to peace and human rights by the United Nations and its strongest member has been largely abandoned. Our neglect of these obligations increases the suffering of the innocent and defenseless.

I am grateful to see our withdrawal of U.S. forces from Iraq, but we are negotiating now to retain between eight thousand and twelve thousand NATO troops in Afghanistan until 2024. The primary impediment to an agreement is our insistence that these troops be immune from prosecution under Afghan law for any crimes they may commit. If the troops remain, their peacekeeping role should be combined with a concerted effort by the United Nations and others to negotiate amicable settlement of disputes.

3 | THE BIBLE AND GENDER EQUALITY

The relegation of women to an inferior or circumscribed status by many religious leaders is one of the primary reasons for the promotion and perpetuation of sexual abuse. If potential male exploiters of women are led to believe that their victim is considered inferior or "different" even by God, they can presume that it must be permissible to take advantage of their superior male status. It is crucial that devout believers abandon the premise that their faith mandates sexual discrimination. Islamic scholars assure me that there is no justification for this discrimination in the Koran, but there are specific verses in the Holy Bible that can be interpreted on either side of the issue, and some ascendant male leaders in all faiths take advantage of the interpretation most beneficial to them. There are now about 7 billion people in the world, and more than 2 billion are Christians. Since many fundamental beliefs about human relationships are common to all major religions, I will assess this issue at some length, from a Christian's point of view.

I have been quite active in my local church and in the Southern Baptist Convention, both before and after I held public office. Like my father before me, I am a deacon and a Bible teacher and have volunteered as a layman to work as a missionary in several states to explain my Christian faith and invite people to become followers of Jesus Christ as their personal savior. These have been some of the most gratifying experiences of my life. I began teaching Bible lessons when I was eighteen years old, as a midshipman at Annapolis. I continued to do so as a farmer, governor, and president, and still fulfill this pleasant duty in my church in Plains whenever I am home on Sundays, about thirty-five times a year. There are usually several hundred visitors who come to hear me teach, representing most of the states and often ten or twenty foreign countries. About a fifth are Baptists; the others are mostly Protestants and Catholics, but there are also some Jews, Muslims, Buddhists, Hindus, and others who do not profess a religious affiliation or belief. I try to apply the lesson texts, about equally divided between the New Testament and the Hebrew text, to modern-day circumstances and events, and encourage open discussion between me and the audience. At times there are disagreements, and I learn a lot about different points of view concerning issues that divide believers.

These points of contention are not between Muslim and Christian, Catholic and Protestant, or Baptist and Episcopal, but are almost always within our own individual faiths or denominations. The schism among Baptists is one example. There have always been theological disputes, but now the most contentious are those that involve everyday life. In the time of the early Christian Church followers questioned whether it was acceptable to eat meat that had been offered to idols, if one had to become a circumcised Jew first before accepting Christ as savior, which apostle spoke with the most authority, and whether Jesus could be both human and divine. Now the debates are more about the status of homosexuals, the use of contraceptives, when it is permissible to resort to abortion, and if some verses in the Bible can be in error or applicable only to the time when they were written. One of the most prevalent and divisive issues is whether or not women are equal to men in the eyes of God.

After intense debates leading up to the annual Southern Baptist assembly in 2000, the newly chosen leaders and a majority of voting delegates made several decisions that caused me concern, relating to the interpretation of the scriptures. I had no doubt about the sincerity and good intentions of the participants, but my wife and I began to question whether our beliefs were compatible with those adopted and later mandated by the Convention. The change that was most troubling to us was an emphasis on a few specific Bible verses about the status of women and how they would be applied in practical terms, including one that called for wives to be "submissive" to their husbands. Let me quote the passage:

> Be subject to one another out of reverence for Christ. Wives, be subject to your husbands as you are to the Lord. For the husband is the head of the wife just as Christ is the head of the church, the body of which he is the Savior. Just as the church is subject to Christ, so also wives ought to be in everything to their husbands. Husbands, love your wives, just as Christ loved the church and gave himself up for her, in order to make her holy by cleansing her with the washing of water by the word, so as to present the church in splendor, without a spot or wrinkle or anything of the kind—yes, so that she may be holy and without blemish. In the same way, husbands should love their wives as they do their own bodies. He who loves his wife loves himself. For no one ever hates his own body, but he nourishes and tenderly cares for it, just as Christ does for the church, because we are members of his body. For this reason a man will leave his father and mother and be joined to his wife, and the two will become one flesh. This is a great mystery, and I am applying it to Christ and the church. Each of you, however, should love his wife as himself, and a wife should respect her husband. (Ephesians 5:21–33)

It seems to me that the first sentence introduces a balanced and equal relationship in marriage, but I understand how male supremacists base their claim on some selected phrases.

When I was a child, the most revered Baptist was Lottie Moon, who had been one of our early missionaries to China. She gave much of her food to poor people and died of starvation. Even now, the financial contribution of Baptist congregations for evangelistic work in foreign countries is given in the name of this woman. In every sense of the word, she was the leader in evangelism, a fundamental commitment of my faith. Although a number of female Baptist pastors had been called by local congregations to serve their churches for many years, in 2000 official actions of the more conservative Southern Baptist Convention leaders soon made it clear that Southern Baptist women would no longer be serving as deacons, pastors, or chaplains in the armed forces, or even as professors in some Convention seminaries if there were male students in the classroom. I felt that another ancient principle was being violated with this decision: the premise that each local Baptist congregation was autonomous and that a majority of those voting in conference had the authority to decide who could join as members and who would serve God as lay leaders or the church's pastor.

Rosalynn and I decided to end our relationship with the denomination to which I had been loyal during the first seventy years of my life, but to remain active in our local Baptist church congregation, which was more traditional in its beliefs. For the same reasons, a substantial number of individual Baptists and entire church congregations made the same decision. There is an obvious need and desire among Baptists to resolve these disagreements, and some progress has been made, but one of the most obvious and persistent differences is whether to accept women in positions of leadership if they are elected by a local congregation. In our own Maranatha Baptist Church we enjoy having both a man and a woman as pastors, and at this time half our elected deacons (including the chair) are women.

Later I will describe how people of other faiths disagree on this issue, but let me first explain why, in my opinion, Jesus Christ was the greatest liberator of women in a society where they had been considered throughout biblical history to be inferior. Even wives and widows of prominent and revered men had few legal rights. It is well known to those familiar with the Bible that, to enhance his own well-being, the patriarch Abraham gave away his wife, Sarah, to live in the harem of the pharaoh of Egypt and later attempted to give her to the heathen king Abimelech, claiming both times that she was not his wife but his sister. Men could possess multiple women (King Solomon had three hundred wives and seven hundred concubines), but a woman could be punished by stoning to death if she had more than one sex partner.

There is one incontrovertible fact concerning the relationship between Jesus Christ and women: he treated them as equal to men, which was dramatically different from the prevailing custom of the times. The four Gospels were written by men, but they never report any instance of Jesus' condoning sexual discrimination or the implied subservience or inferiority of women. In a departure from earlier genealogies, Matthew even includes four gentile women (all of whom had extramarital affairs) among the ancestors of Christ: Tamar, Rahab, Ruth, and Bathsheba. The exaltation of and later devotion to Mary, as Jesus' mother, is a vivid indication of the special status of women in Christian theology.

There are too many examples from the earthly ministry of Christ to describe here, but two or three are illustrative. Despite the strict prohibition against a Jewish man dealing with women in public, Jesus had no hesitancy about conversing at the community well with a Samaritan woman who was a pariah both among Jews and her peers because of her ethnicity and lascivious behavior. She accepted him as the promised Messiah and took his message back to her village—the first example of an evangelical witness. Jesus also rejected the double standard of punishment for adultery, by granting both a pardon and forgiveness to a guilty and condemned woman. Christians remember the story of how Jesus dealt with this ancient but then still prevailing command:

> And the scribes and Pharisees brought unto him a woman taken in adultery; and when they had set her in the midst, they say unto him, "Master, this woman was taken in adul-

tery, in the very act. Now Moses in the law commanded us, that such should be stoned: but what sayest thou?" This they said, tempting him, that they might have to accuse him. But Jesus stooped down, and with his finger wrote on the ground, as though he heard them not. So when they continued asking him, he lifted up himself, and said unto them, "He that is without sin among you, let him first cast a stone at her." And again he stooped down, and wrote on the ground. And they which heard it, being convicted by their own conscience, went out one by one, beginning at the eldest, even unto the last: and Jesus was left alone, and the woman standing in the midst. When Jesus had lifted up himself, and saw none but the woman, he said unto her, "Woman, where are thine accusers? Hath no man condemned thee?" She said, "No man, Lord." And Jesus said unto her, "Neither do I condemn thee: go, and sin no more." (John 8:3–11)

The Gospel of Jesus Christ has at its center the ending of domination of every kind. For some Christians to use the Gospel to compromise the human rights of women and others borders on the obscene. Propagated with appeals to idealized heritage, immutable sacred history, and paternalistic care for the religiously ignorant, their rights-denying actions must be exposed for what they are—formal policies for the retention and augmenting of power by those men who already have it. The ethic of Jesus Christ proclaims the radical equality of human value. The ending of the subordination of women—and of all who are dominated—is critical to the building of the reign of God on earth as it is in heaven.

DR. ALISON BODEN,

DEAN OF RELIGIOUS LIFE, PRINCETON UNIVERSITY

Perhaps more significant was the fact that women traveled with Jesus' entourage and that their spiritual and financial support within his ministry was accepted. It may be that his closest confidante was Mary, the sister of Martha and Lazarus, whom he visited often in Bethany and who seemed to be one of the few people who understood that he would be crucified and resurrected. She anointed his feet with perfume a few days before his death, as Jesus said, "It was intended that she should save this perfume for the day of my burial" (John 12:7). Mary Magdalene, one of his loyal followers, had the honor of visiting his empty tomb; Jesus then appeared to her and instructed her to inform all the other disciples, who were hiding in fear in a secret place, that the Savior was risen from the grave.

There are a few selections from Saint Paul's letters to the early churches that, taken out of historical context, seem to indicate his departure from Jesus' example and show a bias against women by directing that they should be treated as second-class Christians. I do not maintain that these troubling scriptures are in error or that there are contradictions between different portions of the inspired word of God, but it is necessary to assess the local circumstances within troubled early church congregations and interpret Paul's instructions to "brothers and sisters" who were confused and disorderly. Paul is not mandating permanent or generic theological policies when he directs that women worship with their heads covered, keep their hair unbraided, dress modestly, and never adorn themselves or speak in a worship service. In a letter to his disciple Timothy, Paul expresses a prohibition against women teaching men, but we know, and he knew, that Timothy was instructed by his mother and grandmother. It is also difficult to understand how Paul's close friend Priscilla is revered for having been a teacher of Apollos, one of the great evangelists of that day, so that he could more accurately reveal that Jesus was indeed the long-awaited Messiah.

To resolve the apparent disharmony between Jesus and Paul, I refer to some of Paul's remarks. In his letter to the Galatians, he states, "But now that faith has come, we are no longer subject to a disciplinarian, for in Christ Jesus you are all children of God through faith. . . . There is no longer Jew or Greek, there is no longer slave or free, there is no longer male and female; for all of you are one in Christ Jesus." (Galatians 3:25-28) In his letter to the Romans, Paul thanked twenty-eight outstanding leaders of the early churches, at least ten of whom were women: "I commend to you our sister Phoebe, a deacon of the church at Cenchreae. . . . Greet Priscilla and Aquila, who work with me in Christ Jesus. . . . Greet Mary, who has worked very hard among you. . . . Greet Andronicus and Junia, my relatives who were in prison with me; they are prominent among the apostles, and they were in Christ before I was. . . . Greet Philologus, Julia, Nereus and his sister, and Olympas, and all the saints who are with them." (Romans 16) It is inconceivable to me that Paul would encourage and congratulate inspired women who were successful deacons, apostles, ministers, and saints and still be quoted by male chauvinists as a biblical source for excluding women from accepting God's call to serve others in the name of Christ. Paul has not separated himself from the lesson that Jesus taught: that women are to be treated equally in their right to serve God. Devout Christians can find scriptures to justify either side in this debate. The question is whether we evangelical believers in Christ want to abandon His example and exclude a vast array of potential female partners, who are equally devout and responding to God's call.

To a substantial degree, the argument justifying male dominance is based on two reports in Genesis of God's creation of human beings that may seem somewhat contradictory. It was the sixth day of creation when, as described in Genesis 1:26–27, "God said, 'Let us make humankind in our image, according to our likeness. . . .' So God created humankind in his image, in the image of God he created them; male and female he created them." Then, in the second chapter of Genesis, God first created man and later decided that he needed a partner. "So the Lord God caused a deep sleep to fall upon the man, and he slept; then he took one of his ribs and closed up its place with flesh. And the rib that the Lord God had taken from the man he made into a woman and brought her to the man. . . . Therefore a man leaves his father and his mother and clings to his wife, and they become one flesh." Both of these scriptures emphasize the mutuality and equality of worth of male and female, but many Christian and Jewish fundamentalists use the second selection as a basis for their belief in the superiority of men because man was created first. This belief is combined with the allegation that Eve should be held solely accountable for "original sin" because she accepted the forbidden apple from the serpent, tasted it, and gave it to Adam.

My inclination is to consider more seriously the policies of the early Christian Church, after Jesus Christ came to explain the meaning of more ancient texts and to let us know more personally the true nature of God, who exemplifies a combination of justice, mercy, forgiveness, and love. The question of patriarchy is addressed quite clearly in Saint Paul's 1 Corinthians 11:11–12: "You need to learn, however, that woman is not different from man, and man is not different from woman. Woman may come from man, but man is born of woman. And both come from God."

There is no need to argue about such matters, because it is human nature to be both selective and subjective in deriving the most convenient meaning by careful choices from the thirty-one thousand or so verses in the modern Christian Bible. If men with religious authority wish to remain in power, they can accept the version they prefer.

It is ironic that women are now welcomed into ascendant positions in all major professions and other endeavors but are deprived of the right to serve Jesus Christ in positions of leadership as they did during his earthly ministry and for about three centuries in the early Christian churches. It is inevitable that this sustained religious suppression of women as inferior or unqualified has been a major influence in depriving women of equal status within the worldwide secular community as spelled out in the Universal Declaration of Human Rights.

It is likely that Christians and people of other faiths who represent the purest and most admirable qualities of their beliefs are those who devote their lives to service among people in need. When we have gone into the isolated villages throughout Africa to try to control or eliminate debilitating diseases, we have found that the Islamic mullahs, Christian priests, or other spiritual leaders are often providing the only rudimentary medical care available to the community. In the absence of medical training and modern treatment capability, they are dealing with cases of AIDS, encroaching blindness, worms within or emerging from bodies, extended stomachs and stunted growth of children, grossly enlarged arms and legs, open wounds, and broken bones. The religious leaders are the ones most trusted by the people, and, with no confusing theological debates as an impediment, they deal with fellow believers as equal to each other and deserving of blessing from whatever superior being they revere. Their commitment to serving others is inspirational.

In my presidential inaugural address I promised to promote human rights around the world, and later I used the imprisonment and murder of Ugandan people by President Idi Amin as a horrible example of abuse of those rights. The dictator retaliated by ordering all Americans in his country to assemble in Entebbe and threatened them with death or expulsion. I was in a quandary about how to respond, until I learned that he claimed to be a Muslim and was very proud of having made a pilgrimage to Mecca. I called the king of Saudi Arabia to seek his help and was relieved to hear almost immediately an announcement from Amin that the Americans would be permitted to leave Uganda unharmed. The majority of them, who were Christian missionaries, sent me notice that not one of them was accepting this offer but that all would remain at their assigned posts with their families, despite the continuing threats to their lives.

For many generations, religious missionaries have provided a connecting link between worshipers in more affluent communities and less fortunate people who are suffering from hunger, disease, and oppression. There is no distinction between men and women, either among the benefactors or those who receive the benefits of their ministry. It is impossible to overestimate their dedication and the positive impact of religious organizations like the Catholic Relief Services, Heifer International, the International Islamic Charitable Organization, and dozens of others. Religious and secular organizations provide more assistance to needy people than the contributions of governments and they combine financial help with devoted service. They form close personal ties in local communities and recognize the special suffering of women and children from deprivation and abuse, though they are sometimes constrained in their good works by laws and religious tenets that perpetuate sexual discrimination. I serve on the finance committee of our small church in Plains, and 10 percent of our total annual budget is earmarked—without discussion or debate—for the work of Baptist missionaries overseas. We collect a special additional offering each year for those providing benevolent services within the United States. In addition to the personal service of thousands of missionaries, religious groups in the United States contribute more than $8 billion annually for benevolent purposes in these projects overseas.

During the year that I ran for president, Jerome and Joanne Ethridge volunteered to serve as foreign missionaries from our local church. After intensive training in French they were assigned to serve in Togo, a small country in West Africa. Jerome had worked in the fields of an agricultural experiment station near Plains, and neither he nor Joanne had ever addressed an audience even as Bible teachers, so they had a formidable task in spreading the gospel in about a third of the country. Their assigned area was northeast of a river that was almost impossible to cross during the extended rainy season. Instead of preaching to the people, the Ethridges decided to ascertain their greatest needs and attempt to meet them.

Joanne immediately began to learn the local language, Ifè, and was soon teaching the women how to read and write. At the same time, she worked with biblical scholars who were writing the New Testament in the language. As they traveled from village to village, they observed that few of the people had a supply of clean drinking water and depended instead on stagnant ponds that filled during the rainy season. The water became increasingly unfit as the ponds slowly dried up during the rest of the year, and waterborne diseases were prevalent. Baptists in North Carolina donated a well-drilling outfit, and Jerome went to each village and, with local help, bored holes down to the aquifer and installed a pump. This was a slow process, so Joanne usually went to the villages ahead of Jerome, to prepare the people for her husband's arrival and to teach the rudiments of health care to the women. The Ethridges would say simply that they were providing these services in the name of Jesus Christ. When they had enough converts, they helped to organize a local church congregation. Jerome told me that one of their biggest problems was to induce the men to treat women as equals, not having to cover their heads and encouraging them to speak during worship services, and to teach both boys and girls about their new faith.

After working for several years and bringing fresh and healthy water to more than eighty villages, they decided to build a bridge across the raging river. They sent the well-digging equipment to a missionary in nearby Ghana, and Baptists back home agreed to provide reinforcing bars and cement for the bridge. Neither had ever built anything of the kind, but with the help of volunteers they began their project. Rosalynn and I visited them on one of our trips to the area soon after the bridge was finished. It was heavily used by the previously isolated people, who could now reach the rest of their country throughout the year. When Jerome and Joanne retired after twenty-three years in Togo there were more than five thousand new Christians in the area, and their eighty churches each had a local minister. Based on the example set by Jesus, the men and women acted as equals in His service.

Despite sharp differences of opinion about the role of women in positions of religious leadership, people of faith offer the greatest reservoir of justice, charity, and goodwill in alleviating the unwarranted deprivation and suffering of women and girls. This includes popes, imams, bishops, priests, mullahs, traditional leaders, and their followers who search for ideals and inspiration from a higher authority.

The principle of treating others the same way one would like to be treated is echoed in at least twelve religions of the world. "Others" transcend gender, race, class, sexual orientation or caste. Whoever and whatever the "other" is, she has to be treated with dignity, kindness, love, and respect. In African communitarian spirituality, this is well expressed in the Ubuntu religious and ethical ideal of "I am because you are, and since we are, therefore I am"—a mandate based on the reality of our being interconnected and interdependent as creation. Therefore pain caused to one is pain shared by all.

FULATA MOYO, PROGRAM EXECUTIVE,

WOMEN IN CHURCH AND SOCIETY,

WORLD COUNCIL OF CHURCHES

4 | FULL PRISONS AND LEGAL KILLING

As governor, I began to see more clearly that the tacit acceptance of bias, discrimination, and injustice creates an underlying tendency toward violence or abuse in a society, and a culture that results in the disproportionate suffering of women and others who are unable to defend themselves. This harm is magnified when ascendancy of the powerful is combined with religious beliefs that exalt one group of people at the expense of others.

When our family moved into the governor's mansion we found that the servants there, all black, were trusted inmates from the women's prison, and we learned of their unjust treatment under the law. One of our cooks asked to borrow $250, showing me a letter that indicated she could be released with this payment to the local court in her hometown. I investigated the case and found that her husband had been an abusive drunkard who stayed at home only on her paydays as a licensed practical nurse; he beat her and took almost all the money. One day she fought back and killed him with a butcher knife. She nevertheless was sentenced to prison until she paid a fine of $750. As an inmate she had been able to raise only $500 during her past four years in prison. I had the state attorney general intercede, and the woman was set free within a few days.

Rosalynn and I met a woman while vacationing on Cumberland Island, off the Georgia coast, who reported that her mother had borrowed $225 to put up bail for her son, who was charged with a minor crime. She was illiterate and had put her mark on what she understood was a promissory note with her five acres of land as collateral. When she went to repay the loan she was told that she had signed a warranty deed and had sold her land. I went to the Camden County courthouse and found that the report was true, but there was a pending legal case and it would be improper for a governor to intercede. The Georgia Supreme Court later ruled against the woman, and she lost her property.

Another case involved a young woman named Mary Fitzpatrick, who was visiting a friend in the small town of Lumpkin, Georgia. A man was killed in a gunfight, and as the only visitor in town Mary was accused of the crime and taken to jail. She first met her court-appointed lawyer as they entered the courtroom for the trial, and he advised her to plead guilty, with a promise of light punishment. Instead she received a sentence of life imprisonment. Mary demonstrated extraordinary talent in all her assigned duties during our four years in the governor's mansion, and as the newly elected president I obtained permission to act as her parole officer and to take her to the White House with us. In the meantime, the trial judge in Lumpkin had become a member of the Supreme Court of Georgia, and he agreed to have the evidence reexamined. Mary's innocence was proven, and she received a full pardon.

I began to visit the state prisons and found terrible discrimination against poor, black, and mentally handicapped people. Some had been in solitary confinement for several years. I employed a professional criminologist, Ellis C. MacDougall, as the director of Georgia state prisons and initiated an overhaul of our policies. Working with Director MacDougall's guidance, I explored ways to decrease the number of imprisoned citizens. We gave sentenced persons a thorough physical and mental examination to learn their past experience and inherent capability and to ascertain the best education and training programs in prison to prepare them for a productive life. We depended on early release and work-release programs as jail terms neared an end, and I recruited a large corps of probation officers from among members of the Lions, Kiwanis, Rotary, and other service clubs. These volunteers spent a day or two in Atlanta with me and the prisons director and went through an intensive training course. They pledged to accept just one prospective probationer or parolee as a personal responsibility, visited the prisoner's family before release, and promised to find or provide a full-time job for the person in their charge. These volunteers worked closely, of course, with professional probation officers.

These same efforts were being made by other state leaders, and during our annual governors' conferences we shared experiences and competed to determine who had most reduced our prison populations. At a gathering of Georgia's former governors in 1995, Rosalynn asked one of the most recent about his greatest success in office. He proudly replied, "We built enough prison cells to reach from the state capitol to my home town." The construction and operation of local and state prisons has now become a valuable economic asset, especially in more remote rural areas where other industries are scarce.

There is an inevitable chasm between societal leaders who write and administer criminal laws and the people who fill the jails, often unnecessarily. The cumulative effect of this gap is a lowering of barriers against discrimination and violence that affects racial minorities, women, the mentally handicapped, and others who are naturally more helpless and vulnerable. We who are more privileged are not deliberately perpetuating our status at the expense of others, but we rarely wish to confront or be involved in the problem. Exalted commitments to peace and human rights are abandoned as we accept and rationalize the privileges we enjoy. The prison system is just one clear example.

At that time, in the 1970s, only one in a thousand Americans was in prison, but our nation's focus has turned increasingly to punishment, not rehabilitation. During the past three decades extended incarceration of people convicted of drug use and other nonviolent crimes has replaced an emphasis on rehabilitation with job training and restoration of citizens' rights after the convicted have paid their debt to society. There are now more than five times as many American inmates in federal, state, and local prisons as when I was president, and the number of incarcerated black women has increased by 800 percent! An ancillary effect is that this increased incarceration has come at a tremendous financial cost to taxpayers, at the expense of education and other beneficial programs. The cost of prosecuting executed criminals is astronomical. Since 1973, California alone has spent roughly $4 billion in capital cases, leading to only thirteen executions, amounting to about $307 million spent for the killing of each prisoner.

Although the number of violent crimes has not increased, the United States has the highest incarceration rate in the world, with more than 7.43 per 1,000 adults imprisoned at the end of 2010. With only 4.5 percent of the world's population, we claim 22 percent of the world's prison population. Many of these prisoners, some now incarcerated for life, have never been found guilty of a violent crime but have been convicted of drug-related offenses. The American Civil Liberties Union reported in November 2013 that there are now 3,278 persons in federal and state prisons who are serving life sentences without parole—for nonviolent crimes! Not surprisingly, 65.4 percent of them are black. I gave a major address about drug use while president in 1979 and called for the decriminalization of marijuana, but not its legalization, with an emphasis on treatment and not imprisonment for users who were not involved in the distribution of narcotics. This proposal was well received at the time, but the emphasis was placed on punishment and not rehabilitation after I left office.

Despite the proliferation of excessive imprisonments, the number of pardons by U.S. presidents has also been dramatically reduced. I issued 534 pardons in my four-year term, and in their eight-year terms Ronald Reagan issued 393, Bill Clinton 396, and George W. Bush 189, but in his first term Barack Obama issued only 23.

⟨∞⟩

As a "Nun on the Bus" I heard the struggles of ordinary
people. I learned that to be pro-life (and not just pro-birth)
we must create a world where all people have their basic
needs met. This is justice. Governments hold the responsibility of enacting laws that ensure living wages and safety nets
for people who fall through the cracks of the economy. In
the United States, both federal and state policy makers must
end political gridlock and enact just laws that ensure that
all people have access to the basics: food, shelter, education,
healthcare, and living wages. These are pro-life programs.

SISTER SIMONE CAMPBELL OF NUNS ON THE BUS

In October 2013 the United Nations special rapporteur on violence
against women, Rashida Manjoo, reported a substantial increase in
the proportion of women being incarcerated globally compared to men,
and stated that conditions of their imprisonment are more severe than
those faced by men. She explained that women often are subjected to
incarceration for crimes committed under coercion from men who exercise abusive authority over them, especially in the pursuit of illegal
drug trafficking or other criminal enterprises. "Moral crimes," such as
sex outside of marriage, are additional reasons for incarcerating women
that do not affect men, and they face stringent evidentiary rules that
even result in punishment of rape victims. Conditions in prison can
also be more severe for women, as they face increased risk of sexual
assault. Manjoo also addressed the issue of young children living in
prisons with their mothers, as well as the situation of women who are
primary caretakers of children and the devastating effects of their detention on children left behind.

The special rapporteur stated, "Current domestic and international
anti-drug policies are one of the leading causes of rising rates of incarceration of women around the world. . . . In a context of scarce resources and, given that most women offenders rarely pose a threat to

the public, it is imperative that States consider alternatives to women's incarceration."

Another significant and extraordinary response to crime in the United States and other countries is the death penalty. The Carter Center takes a firm stand against capital punishment, and I often send a letter to foreign leaders under whose authority people are sentenced to death. Rosalynn and I also intercede with U.S. governors and others who may be able to commute the ultimate punishment to life imprisonment.

In a case before the U.S. Supreme Court while I was governor in 1972, *Furman v. Georgia*, the justices issued a de facto moratorium on capital punishment throughout the United States because there were no clear and consistent legal grounds for its imposition. An important question was whether the death penalty was a violation of the U.S. Constitution, which prohibits "cruel and unusual" punishment. When all the states complied with new standards, the Court permitted the resumption of executions in 1976 as a result of *Gregg v. Georgia* and similar cases from other states. There were just three state executions in the United States while I was governor and president, one in 1977 and two in 1979, but there have been 1,359 since 1980. It is interesting that there have been only three executions by the federal government since 1976.

The United States is the only country in NATO or North America that still executes its citizens, and Belarus and Suriname are the only exceptions in Europe and South America. In fact, the Charter of Fundamental Rights of the European Union specifically prohibits the death penalty among any of its members. Even with a strongly conservative U.S. Supreme Court, there have been encouraging signs that decisions made in other Western democracies and changing American public opinion are having an effect. In 2002 the Court ruled that an "intellectually disabled" person could not be executed; in 2005 the death penalty was not permitted for criminals under the age of eighteen; and in 2008 it was prohibited for rape if no death was involved.

Unfortunately, individual states are still permitted to define "intellectually disabled," and some of them, including Georgia and Florida, make it almost impossible to legally meet the criteria, so that people who are severely handicapped are killed.

It is clear that there are overwhelming ethical, financial, and religious reasons to abolish this brutal and irrevocable punishment. Although a majority of Americans express support for the death penalty if asked simply if they wish to abolish it altogether, definitive recent polls show that, when given a choice, only 33 percent of Americans would choose the death penalty for murder, while 61 percent would prefer a punishment other than the death penalty. The highest number supports a life sentence without parole plus restitution to the family of the victim. Just 1 percent of police chiefs believe that expanding the death penalty would reduce violent crime. This change in public opinion is steadily restricting capital punishment in state legislatures and the federal courts.

One argument made by proponents of the death penalty is that it is a strong deterrent to murder and other violent crimes, but evidence shows just the opposite. Whereas the last execution in Canada took place in 1962, in 2011 there were 598 murders in Canada and 14,610 in the United States. In fact, the homicide rate is nearly three times greater in the United States than in any Western European country, all without the death penalty. Southern states carry out over 80 percent of executions but have a higher murder rate than any other region. Texas has by far the most executions. Looking at similar adjacent states, there are more capital crimes in South Dakota, Connecticut, and Virginia (with death sentences) than in neighboring North Dakota, Massachusetts, and West Virginia (without death penalties). There has never been any evidence that the death penalty reduces capital crimes or that crimes increased when executions stopped. In fact, in a study conducted by Professor Gary Potter at Eastern Kentucky University, it was found that homicide rates increase before, during, and immediately after executions. This demonstrates that more people become victimized by lethal violence when the state kills. Here is an excerpt from Potter's testimony to the Health and Welfare Committee of the Kentucky legislature in March 1999:

> Studies of capital punishment have consistently shown that homicide actually increases in the time period surrounding an execution. Social scientists refer to this as the "brutalization effect." Execution stimulates homicides in three ways: (1) executions desensitize the public to the immorality of killing, increasing the probability that some people will be motivated to kill; (2) the state legitimizes the notion that vengeance for past misdeeds is acceptable; and (3) executions also have an imitation effect, where people actually follow the example set by the state. After all, people feel if the government can kill its enemies, so can they.

It is logical that any increase in societal violence will increase the incidence of violence against women. When the state acts in a brutal and lethal manner, this conveys to the community that violence is acceptable.

And tragic mistakes are prevalent. DNA testing and other factors have caused 143 death sentences to be reversed since I left the governor's office. Some devout Christians are among the most fervent advocates of the death penalty, contradicting Jesus Christ and misinterpreting Holy Scriptures and numerous examples of mercy. We remember God's forgiveness of Cain, who killed Abel, and the adulterer King David, who arranged the killing of Uriah, the husband of Bathsheba, his lover. Jesus dramatically forgave an adulterous woman sentenced to be stoned to death and explained away the "eye for an eye" scripture. There is a stark difference between Protestant and Catholic believers. Many Protestant leaders are in the forefront of demanding the ultimate punishment, while official Catholic policy condemns the death penalty.

Perhaps the strongest argument against the death penalty is extreme bias in its use against the poor, minorities, and those with diminished mental capacity. Although homicide victims are six times more likely to be black than white, 77 percent of death penalty cases involve white victims. Also, it is hard to imagine a rich white person going to the death chamber after being defended by expensive lawyers. This demonstrates a higher value placed on the lives of white Americans. The prevalence of punishment instead of a chance for rehabilitation is another vivid indication of societal resort to violence, which sets an unintended basis for violence against those who are relatively defenseless.

One hundred forty-three countries have abolished the death penalty by law or in practice, and the United Nations General Assembly has adopted resolutions in 2007, 2008, and 2010 calling for a global moratorium on executions, with a view to eventual abolition. Our country is not in good company in its fascination with the death penalty; 90 percent of all executions are carried out in China, Iran, Saudi Arabia, and the United States.

If the idea is to end violence in society, then killing is certainly not the answer.

DIVYA IYER, SENIOR RESEARCHER AT
AMNESTY INTERNATIONAL IN INDIA

As everyone knows, young people are bombarded with "normalized" violence through highly realistic video games that take the player through many hours of simulated combat and criminal behavior. In addition, movies, television, magazines, and music videos are full of demeaning depictions of women. These games and media make us less sensitive to violence and the debasement of women, so we are more inclined to accommodate them in real life.

Despite these disturbing trends toward a more violent global society, it is reassuring that our most notable heroes, even in more modern times, have remained the champions of peace, including Mahatma Gandhi, Mother Teresa, Martin Luther King Jr., and Nelson Mandela.

5 | SEXUAL ASSAULT AND RAPE

Although I am not a lawyer, I have been involved in the drafting, passage, and implementation of laws on almost every conceivable subject as a legislator, governor, and president. I was closest to law enforcement while governor, riding always in the front passenger seat of a State Patrol car and often assuming the duties of a radioman. There were a few times when I approved the driver's request to run down a speeding vehicle or to investigate a suspicious incident that we witnessed.

While Rosalynn and I were living in the governor's mansion we had a young out-of-state college student stay with us for a brief period early in the fall semester, until she could get settled in a dormitory. After attending class for a few days she came home one night and woke us, crying, to report that she had been raped. We called a doctor to examine her; he found several serious bruises on her arms and around her genitals and prescribed a sedative so she could get some sleep. The next morning I asked our guest if she knew her rapist, and she replied that he was a fellow classmate with whom she had decided to go on a date. At my urging, she agreed that I report the crime, and when I arrived at my office I called the state's attorney, reported the incident, and asked that he proceed with legal action.

He reported late that afternoon that he was having some difficulty, and I was infuriated to learn that the local officials were reluctant to make a legal issue of the case. I directed them to come see me. Quite apologetically, the officials said that this was a fairly common occurrence on university campuses, that the attacker always claimed that sex was consensual, and that any case brought against a white male student had very little chance of success. In addition, the young woman would be forced to testify in a highly publicized trial and would be cross-examined about every detail of the events during the date night and any other sexual experiences she might have had in the past. He added that it was the general policy of the two dozen colleges and universities in the Atlanta area to resort to counseling of both parties instead of a court trial. With permission of our young guest, I discussed the issue with her parents, and they decided that she should enroll in a different college.

I have been a distinguished professor at Emory University for the past thirty-two years, and in addition to teaching and lecturing I meet regularly with the president, deans, and other professors to discuss mutual interests of The Carter Center and Emory. I told the president about our guest at the governor's mansion and deplored the policy of many universities to resort to counseling of both victim and rapist and to punish or expel a male student only in egregious cases or when there was clear proof of repetitive offenses. He expressed concern at how infrequently the survivors of sexual assault choose to go down the hard road of legal recourse and explained that Emory had recently established a new policy to deal with this problem, with a separate process for sexual assault.

Administrators, faculty, and student leaders at Emory are evolving plans to promulgate more widely the warnings of and penalties for sexual abuse, train a permanent cadre of one thousand sexual assault peer advocates, encourage immediate reporting of abuse by victims and bystanders, provide private and professional counseling for victims, and decide what legal steps to take against students found guilty of rape. With the help of experts like Dr. David Lisak, a forensic consultant, Emory and other universities are learning how they can increase students' confidence in an effective administration of justice. Dr. Lisak's research focuses on "the causes and consequences of interpersonal violence—motives and behaviors of rapists and murderers." It has been estimated that one in five female students is sexually assaulted in American universities, but most people do not know that most of these crimes are premeditated and committed by a few men. This problem is perpetuated by the reluctance of rape victims to report the crime and to identify the perpetrator, who is almost always known to the victim before the attack. One of the reasons for this reluctance is a lack of clear procedures and support structures on the campus, and many college administrators are reluctant to address the problem because of the potential stigma to the institution if there is an increase in reported sexual assault cases. Another group reluctant to resolve cases of sexual assault is other men who witness or learn about the attack and know who the rapists are. They have to be convinced of its seriousness, become acquainted with campus policy, and be willing to support the victim instead of the criminal.

A report funded by the U.S. Justice Department found that more than 95 percent of students who are sexually assaulted remain silent, a much larger proportion than among the general public. The report's analysis, conducted at the State University of New York in New Paltz, revealed that an institution of that size, with about eight thousand students, would be expected to have more than 1,700 female victims of rape or sexual assault during the eleven years of the study. However, only six students reported a sexual assault to the office responsible for initiating proceedings, and only three cases resulted in a campus hearing—with one male student expelled.

The tragedy is that most on-campus rapes are perpetrated by serial rapists, who can safely assume that their crimes will not be revealed. In a New England study published in 2002 in the journal *Violence and Victims*, 120 rapists were identified among a sample of 1,882 students.

Of those, seventy-six were serial rapists who had each, on average, left fourteen seriously scarred victims. Their collective tally included 439 rapes and attempted rapes, 49 sexual assaults, 343 acts of sexual abuse or violence against children, and 214 acts of battery against intimate partners. In most cases their crimes were planned and premeditated. Why would any institution want them to remain as students? One answer comes from the *Hopkins Undergraduate Research Journal* of March 2012, which reported that one in three college assaults that get reported are committed by student athletes, who are often popular and influential.

Despite institutional unwillingness to deal forcefully with these crimes, there is increasing legal pressure to do so from an unexpected source. Title IX of the Education Amendments to the Civil Rights Act became effective in 1972 and is widely known for its prevention of discrimination against female students in campus sports. In 2001 the law was interpreted by the Department of Education to apply to sexual harassment, and now schools are required to designate a coordinator for Title IX and to take "immediate and appropriate steps to investigate or otherwise determine what occurred and take prompt and effective steps to end any harassment, eliminate a hostile environment if one has been created, and prevent harassment from occurring again." The threat of having federal funds withheld is a powerful incentive for an institution to comply, and I hope the U.S. Department of Education will put maximum pressure on schools at all levels to establish policies that are firm and clear. With proper leadership at the presidential level, universities can prevent deans and other officials from responding to a report of rape simply by suggesting the victim get counseling or take some time off or by telling her that legal proceedings are likely to embarrass her and result only rarely in punishment for the rapist.

Emory University is moving rapidly to evolve a balanced and effective policy of dealing with the problem of sexual assaults on its female students, and the student body seems to be supportive. This is one comment about an early progress report that appeared in the student newspaper:

"Emory has failed to enact sanctions that are capable of deterring would-be perpetrators. In the context of the existing sexual misconduct policy, there are no written sanctions listed for perpetrators. Creating a more stringent policy does more than just add another line to the University's sexual misconduct policy. It will raise awareness of the intolerable nature of sexual assault and start to reduce the number of attacks on our campus. Ultimately and most importantly, we can create an environment that makes it more likely for victims to come forward and take action against those who have sexually assaulted them, as well as put in place a strong deterrent against such crimes being committed in the first place."

It's time for all people of faith to be outraged. It's time for our Christian leaders to stand up and say that women, made in the very image of God, deserve better. And it's time for us in the faith community to acknowledge our complicity in a culture that too often not only remains silent, but also can propagate a false theology of power and dominance. There is a growing understanding that women must be central to shaping solutions. . . . There is a new generation of young leaders determined to ensure the bright future of all people regardless of gender.

JIM WALLIS,

AUTHOR, FOUNDER AND EDITOR OF

Sojourners MAGAZINE

When I was serving in the Naval Reserve Officers Training Corps program at Georgia Tech, as a midshipman at Annapolis, and on battleships and submarines, it was understood that the role of women in the military was limited to service in the continental United States and that their duties would be in medical professions, communications, intelligence, science and technology, and as storekeepers. For all practical purposes, they were given equal status in January 2013, when the secretary of defense announced that the ban on women serving in combat roles would be lifted. The most recent report is that women now make up 14 percent of U.S. military personnel, with more than 165,000 enlisted and 35,000 women serving as officers.

I was pleased when the decision was made while I was president to appoint women as Naval Academy midshipmen with equal status. Rosalynn and I are usually invited to spend a few nights with the superintendent during visits to the campus for my class reunions, and we have listened with close attention to descriptions of how much progress has been made in successfully assimilating women midshipmen, now about 22 percent of the total student population, into life in the enormous Bancroft Hall dormitory, in public activities, in the classrooms, and on ships.

I have learned, however, that my alma mater has the same basic policy concerning sexual assaults as other institutions of higher education, and this permissive policy is now being questioned since a female midshipman alleged that she was gang-raped by three football players during a party at an off-campus house in April 2012. The female cadet said she got drunk at the party and passed out. She had little recollection of what had happened but learned about the alleged assault from friends and social media. She said she felt tremendous pressure not to report the incident. After she did bring the case to naval authorities, she stopped fully cooperating with them, still fearing a backlash. Later, her lawyer explained that she "was ostracized and retaliated against by the football players and the Naval Academy community." She was punished for underage drinking while her accused assailants were allowed to keep playing football. The Naval Criminal Investigative Service closed the initial investigation.

The female cadet sought legal help and the Navy reopened the investigation. In August 2013 an official hearing was conducted, with the purpose of making a report to the Academy superintendent, who would then decide whether to put the case into the hands of prosecutors and law enforcement officials in military court. As I was writing this on a Saturday morning during the hearing, the news media reported that the twenty-one-year-old female midshipman had requested a respite for the weekend after being cross-examined for more than twenty hours during the past three days, enduring waves of hostile questions from lawyers of the accused. The officer presiding over the hearing denied her request, stating that he couldn't excuse her as long as she was physically able to testify. She explained that she had refused to cooperate with investigators at first because she was scared of what might happen to her and because she didn't want her mother to find out that she had been raped. The previous day's interrogation had focused on her technique in performing oral sex. "How wide did you open your mouth?" the lawyer asked. He claimed it was a linchpin of his client's defense, as were questions about her previous love affairs and the type of underwear she wore.

No court-martial has begun against any of the football players yet, but charges in the sexual assault case were dropped against two of the football players, one in January 2014 because he had not been read his rights before questioning. At the same time, it was reported by the Pentagon that during the past year the Air Force Academy had reported forty-five cases of sexual assault, with fifteen reported cases at the Naval Academy and ten at West Point. Senator Kirsten E. Gillibrand, Democrat of New York, released a statement on January 10 saying that "the prevalence of sexual assault in the military and the crisis of underreporting continue to extend to the academies, and that is tragic and heartbreaking."

This almost inconceivable procedure at the U.S. Naval Academy—with prosecution of the alleged rapists entirely up to the commanding officer—demonstrates vividly why victims of rape in the military are so reluctant to report the assaults. In addition, the U.S. Justice Department utilizes this fear of reporting abuse as a means to excuse the Department of Veterans Affairs from paying rape victims when later medical claims are made. As reported by Ruth Marcus of the *Washington Post* in October 2013, U.S. appellate judges have ruled in several cases that female victims, after release from the military, are not eligible for financial help for psychiatric or other damages unless they had reported the crime immediately after it occurred. Despite the fact that the military acknowledges that most rapes and other serious sexual assaults are never reported to authorities and that severe permanent damage, including post-traumatic stress disorder, often requires treatment for victims in later years, these rulings specify that failure to make a timely report of these crimes can be used as evidence that they did not occur. Marcus summarizes, "In short, we know these incidents are not reported, yet if you don't report them, you're out of luck."

Lawmakers in Congress have proposed taking the decision-making power to press charges in sexual assault cases out of the military chain of command and putting it into the hands of prosecutors and law enforcement professionals. This question was raised after the Department of Defense estimated that there were about 26,000 instances of unwanted sexual contact in the military in 2012 (up from 19,000 two years earlier), but, according to Pentagon statistics, only about 3,200 assaults were reported and 300 prosecuted, which is about 1.2 percent of known cases. This tiny number of prosecutions, and much fewer convictions, can be compared with about 37 percent of prosecutions for similar crimes in the civilian court system.

I know from personal experience in the Navy that commanding officers are responsible for ensuring appropriate protection and care of victims, as well as for investigating and holding accountable those who have committed crimes. I also know that it reflects negatively on commanders' leadership capabilities if such misconduct is known to exist among their subordinates. It was reported to Congress that two male officers among the rare offenders convicted by courts-martial of sexual assault were given clemency by three-star generals. Instead of accepting the proposal to remove total control of military commanders from prosecution, Congress passed legislation in December 2013 that will tighten responses to cases of rape and sexual assault by ending the statute of limitations, barring military commanders from overturning jury convictions, making it a crime to retaliate against people who report such crimes, mandating dishonorable discharge or dismissal of anyone convicted of such crimes, and giving civilian defense officials more control over prosecutions.

This is notable progress, but the problem is much more serious among American troops than is generally acknowledged. According to a report by National Public Radio in 2010, "a survey of female veterans found that 30 percent said they were raped in the military. A 2004 study of veterans who were seeking help for post-traumatic stress disorder found that 71 percent of the women said they were sexually assaulted or raped while serving. And a 1995 study of female veterans of the Gulf and earlier wars, found that 90 percent had been sexually harassed." It was reported more recently that some women employees of civilian contractors serving in a war zone must sign an agreement that forbids them from suing if they are raped by a fellow worker.

The lesson to be learned from all this is how prevalent the rape of women is in universities and the military, two of the most appreciated and revered sectors of American society, where sexual equality is guaranteed and our respected government professes to honor the highest standards of justice. We can only imagine how much worse the situation can be in nations where women are officially derogated and where civil war zones are known to be completely lawless.

Earlier I asserted that the normalization of violence committed by the state encourages violence in society, and this idea especially applies to young people in the military and in universities. If our military is called upon to commit unjustified violence, this will influence the thinking and behavior of highly impressionable service members and college students, who are just beginning to live independently and exert themselves in a highly charged environment. If their government easily chooses violence and punishment to solve problems, they will internalize this choice, which will influence how they deal with each other and make their own way in the world.

There is sometimes encouraging public concern about excessive leniency in civilian courts toward rapists and a lack of concern about victims. It has been demonstrated in Montana, when a fifty-four-year-old teacher, Stacey Rambold, raped one of his fourteen-year-old students, who subsequently committed suicide. Rambold was initially ordered to complete a sexual offender treatment program. However, when Rambold violated the terms of the program, he was brought back to court for sentencing by District Judge G. Todd Baugh. At the sentencing hearing, the judge stated that the rape victim was "older than her chronological age" and was "probably as much in control of the situation" as her rapist, and sentenced Rambold to fifteen years, but suspended all but thirty days to be served in prison. The judge's action is alleged to have violated a Montana state law specifying a minimum of two years' imprisonment for this offense. Members of the National Organization for Women filed a complaint with the Montana Judicial Standards Commission, which has the power to sanction jurists. Petitions with over 140,000 signatures accompanied their complaint calling for removal of the judge from the bench. This altercation has not yet been resolved.

Rape trials are extremely sensitive, and care must be taken in making any kind of executive declaration. One unexpected impediment to the all too rare prosecution of accused rapists in the military occurred when President Barack Obama, as commander-in-chief, made a justified comment in May 2013 that those who commit sexual assault should be "prosecuted, stripped of their positions, court-martialed, fired, and dishonorably discharged." Almost immediately more than a dozen pending cases of sexual assault were challenged by both judges and defense lawyers on the grounds that there had been "unlawful command influence," prejudicing the chance for a fair trial for accused rapists. A former judge advocate general of the Army and dean of a law school in Kansas said, "His remarks were more specific than I've ever heard from a commander-in-chief. When the commander-in-chief says they will be dishonorably discharged, that's a pretty specific message. Every military defense counsel will make a motion about this." As predicted, during the following month charges were dismissed and judges ruled against discharge in cases at Shaw Air Force Base in South Carolina, at Fort Bragg in North Carolina, and in two cases in Hawaii. There have been defense motions with the same allegation in a number of other cases on which final judicial decisions have not yet been made. I remember similar cases that involved the same jurisdictions when I was in the White House, but not being a lawyer I was warned repeatedly by my legal advisors against any interference, no matter how well-intentioned, that might prejudice a jury.

These continuing and largely unresolved sexual crimes in the universities and military branches of America are vivid and disturbing indications of how far we still have to go in protecting some of our most vulnerable citizens. There is a strong reluctance by responsible leaders to admit that such abuses exist within their institutions, and many victims are hesitant about becoming involved in seeking justice, with the prospect of further embarrassment and failure to see the perpetrators punished. Full use of Title IX restraints in educational institutions and action by the Congress regarding abuses in the military can help to reduce these offenses and set an example for other nations.

6 | VIOLENCE AND WAR

One of the first projects adopted by The Carter Center was to identify and honor the world's foremost contributor to human rights each year. An accompanying award of $100,000 was made possible by the generosity of Dominique de Menil, an heiress of the fortune derived from the world's largest petroleum services company, Schlumberger Limited. The ceremonies for the Carter-Menil Human Rights Prize were usually at The Carter Center or the Rothko Chapel in Houston and included an address by Nelson Mandela or another invited guest. I had this honor for the first ceremony, and Dominique asked that I speak about war being the greatest cause of human suffering and abuse, especially of women, children, and others who are innocent and defenseless.

This brought back memories of my early career and my inauguration week at the White House, when Rosalynn and I had a series of receptions for special groups. We were most favorably impressed when the commissioned and noncommissioned military officers came through the receiving line. I was not surprised that, unlike other guests, their comments frequently referred to a hope or prayer for peace. As a naval officer I had been fully prepared for armed combat and believed that by participating in deterring military action against my country I was helping to maintain peace. I had given a lot of thought, both then and when I was serving in elective public office with enormous influence, to the conditions under which it would be appropriate to go to war. My training in military history taught me that in more modern warfare, when there are no clearly defined battle lines in combat as there were in the American Civil War or World War I, it is impossible to discriminate between military and civilian casualties.

When is a war justified? I attempted to answer this question in my speech at the Nobel Peace Prize ceremony as the United States was preparing to launch a second war in Iraq. I did not know at the time that the American president and the British prime minister had decided almost a year earlier to find a justification for the invasion of Iraq. In March 2003, with the invasion imminent, I wanted to address the military action by reiterating the ancient Christian standards for armed combat, and I prepared this op-ed for publication in the *New York Times*:

Just *War*, or a *Just* War?

Profound changes have been taking place in American foreign policy, reversing consistent bi-partisan commitments that for more than two centuries have earned our nation's greatness. These have been predicated on basic religious principles, respect for international law, and alliances that resulted in wise decisions and mutual restraint. Our apparent determination to launch a war against Iraq, without international support, is a violation of these premises.

As a Christian and as a president who was severely provoked by international crises, I became thoroughly familiar with the principles of a just war, and it is clear that a substantially unilateral attack on Iraq does not meet these standards. This is an almost universal conviction of religious leaders, with the most notable exception of a few spokesmen of the Southern Baptist Convention who are greatly influenced by their commitment to Israel based on eschatological (final days) theology.

The preeminent criterion for a just war is that it can only be waged as a last resort, with all non-violent options exhausted. It is obvious that clear alternatives do exist, as previously proposed by our leaders and approved by the United Nations. But now, with our own national security not directly threatened and despite the overwhelming opposition of most people and governments in the world, the United States seems determined to carry out military and diplomatic action that is almost unprecedented in the history of civilized nations. The first stage of our widely publicized war plan is to launch 3000 bombs and missiles on a relatively defenseless Iraqi population within the first few hours of an invasion, with the purpose of so damaging and demoralizing the people that they will change their obnoxious leader, who will most likely be hidden and safe during the massive bombardment.

Weapons used in war must discriminate between combatants and non-combatants. Extensive aerial bombardment, even with precise accuracy, always results in great "collateral damage." The American field commander, General Franks, is complaining in advance about many of the military targets being near hospitals, schools, mosques, and private homes.

Violence used in the war must be proportional to the injury suffered. Despite Saddam Hussein's other serious crimes, American efforts to tie Iraq to the 9/11 terrorist attacks have been unconvincing.

The attackers must have legitimate authority sanctioned by the society they profess to represent. The unanimous vote of approval in the Security Council to eliminate Iraq's weapons of mass destruction can still be honored, but our announced goals are now to achieve regime change and to establish a Pax Americana in the region, perhaps occupying the ethnically divided country for as long as a decade. For these objectives, we do not have international authority. Other members of the U.N. Security Council have so far resisted the enormous economic and political influence that is being exerted from Washington, and we are faced with the possibility of either a failure to get the necessary votes or else a veto from Russia, France, or China. Although Turkey may still be enticed by enormous financial rewards and partial future control of the Kurds and oil in Northern Iraq, its Democratic parliament has at least added its voice to the worldwide expressions of concern.

The peace to be established must be a clear improvement over what exists. Although there are visions of a panacea of peace and democracy in Iraq, it is quite possible that the aftermath of a successful military invasion will destabilize the region, and that aroused terrorists might detract from the personal safety of our people and the security of our nation. Also, to defy overwhelming world opposition will threaten a deep and permanent fracture of the United Nations as a viable institution for world peace.

The heartfelt sympathy and friendship offered to us after the 9/11 terrorist attacks, even from formerly antagonistic regimes, has been largely dissipated, and increasingly unilateral and domineering policies have brought our country to its lowest level of international distrust and antagonism in memory. We will surely decline further in stature if we launch a war in clear defiance of U.N. opposition, but to continue using the threat of our military power to force Iraq's compliance with all U.N. resolutions—with war as a final option—will enhance our status as a champion of peace and justice.

Despite this and other pleas for constraint, we launched a war based on false premises that devastated Iraq, had no beneficial results, and greatly strengthened radical forces in Iran and throughout the region. A total of 4,487 U.S. soldiers have been killed and, according to the British *Lancet*, over 600,000 Iraqis, most of them civilians, had died by June 2006. U.S. armed forces continue to be engaged in a war in Afghanistan that is now in its thirteenth year.

There are times when the international community can work in concert to prevent atrocities and when the use of military force is justified. In Libya in 2011 and again in eastern Congo in 2013, concerted global action, approved by the UN, was taken when atrocities were occurring or threatening.

Mothers and women have suffered serious consequences from the war in Iraq. Increased rates of birth defects have, according to our research, been caused by chemical and radiological contaminants derived from depleted uranium munitions. This affects the future of everyone in our city. The international community must recognize the existence of the problem, acknowledge its size and impact, and offer effective solutions. We need immediate measures to clean the environment and provide necessary resources for the diagnosis and treatment of the many cases of congenital deformity (heart defects) that are occurring. Then the international community must focus on the most important goal of preventing more wars and banning the use of prohibited weapons.

DR. SAMIRA ALAANI,

PEDIATRICIAN, FALLUJAH HOSPITAL, IRAQ

In 2002 the U.S. president announced a military doctrine of "preventive" war, which justifies armed attack or invasion of another country if it is believed that we might be threatened sometime in the future. The "war on terror" was initiated in response to the horrendous attack on the World Trade Center and Pentagon on September 11, 2001, and has no end in sight. We have assumed the right to incarcerate foreign nationals at Guantánamo and within the United States for indefinite periods (possibly for life) without a trial or legal charges being brought against them.

Another example of this unprecedented assumption of unilateral authority to take military action is the execution of suspected evildoers, even American citizens, in foreign countries by drones or Special Forces. Human Rights Watch investigated a series of U.S. drone attacks in Yemen and reported in October 2013 that a disturbing number of the people killed were civilians. At the same time, Amnesty International assessed attacks in Pakistan and estimated that there had been as many as 374 drone strikes since 2004. These two human rights organizations reached a similar conclusion: that hundreds of civilians have been killed and that the United States may have violated international law and even committed war crimes. A separate investigation by UN officials found that 2,200 people have been killed by U.S. drones in Pakistan during the past decade, of whom at least six hundred were either civilians or noncombatants. The nonpartisan New America Foundation, which has a reputation for careful analysis, reports that between 336 and 391 civilians have been killed in Pakistan and Yemen. After these revelations, a pledge was made by the president that new policies would be implemented to make civilian casualties almost impossible. But a drone strike in Yemen in December 2013 targeted an eleven-vehicle convoy—many more vehicles than Al Qaeda would typically use—that turned out to be a wedding party traveling to the bride's home. Top Yemeni officials acknowledged that civilians were killed and awarded compensation to the victims' families: about $110,000 and 101 Kalashnikov rifles! Such compensation seems to imply that although each death is a tragedy, the total number is not as important as trying to balance America's status as a champion of human rights with deterring terrorist activity.

This is not a new problem. Secret efforts by the United States to kill foreign leaders was a burning issue while I was running for president in 1976, centered on a U.S. Senate committee study conducted under Senator Frank Church (one of my opponents). Because of aroused public condemnation of the practice, President Gerald Ford prohibited assassinations by any agent of the United States, and I later strengthened this directive. It was clear to me that such a program of assassination, except in cases where the action was absolutely necessary to prevent an imminent attack against our nation, was both immoral and counterproductive.

As information becomes available about the "targeted killing" program, mostly carried out by drone strikes, we are learning that the results may be the opposite of what our government hopes to achieve. Two Yemeni citizens traveled in 2013 to Washington, D.C., one to testify before a Senate Judiciary Committee and the other to meet with policymakers. They both came to seek answers about drone strikes that devastated their villages and families. Faisal bin Ali Jaber was the uncle of an imam who was meeting with Al Qaeda members, trying to persuade them to leave terrorism behind, when he was killed in a drone strike that also killed the Al Qaeda members who must have been the target of the strike. Farea Al-Muslimi, who testified before the Senate committee, had been educated in the United States and was a sort of "goodwill ambassador" to Yemen, seeking to convince Yemenis to work together with the United States to root out Al Qaeda from their country. One week before his testimony his village was struck by a drone missile. He told the senators, who listened intently, that support for Al Qaeda has grown since this attack and their recruiting efforts have been more successful than ever before.

One of our 2013 Human Rights Defenders Forum participants, Mossarat Qadeem of Pakistan, works with mothers of radicalized youths, with the goal of helping the youths leave Al Qaeda and the

Taliban. By appealing to their religious beliefs and a positive inter-pretation of the Koran, she has helped ninety-two young men return to productive lives. After the drone strikes, however, her job became much more difficult. Many of their relatives regard these radicals as patriotic heroes fighting against an America that is insensitive to their personal needs and national sovereignty.

It is difficult to envision how our country can regain its commitment to human rights if we remain entangled in permanent global warfare, even if it is supposed to be in the shadows. In retaliation for drone strikes in Pakistan, leading politicians there have exposed the identity of our top CIA officials in Islamabad, resulting in their replacement and heightened tensions between our two governments. There is no way to maintain secrecy with the explosion of communications tech-nology and the eagerness of people to speak out about what they con-sider to be injustice.

International bombing raids and missile attacks on cities engender casualties involving many women, children, and elderly, and in civil wars too it is impossible to concentrate destruction just on soldiers serving in military forces. In addition, there has always been ancillary abuse, especially of women, when the inherent brutality of war tends to remove normal inhibitions that restrain potential rapists and others who assault the weak and vulnerable. This was demonstrated vividly by Japanese soldiers in Korea and China during the 1930s and 1940s and is a source of major concern at this time in eastern Congo and in other areas of combat by militia groups. Even within civilian populations, the acceptance of violence as a normal course of action is a special cause of additional abuse of women and girls.

7 | OBSERVATIONS AS A TRAVELER

My mother was serving in the Peace Corps in India at the age of seventy, contributing her services as a registered nurse. She was stationed in the small village of Vikhroli, near Bombay (now Mumbai), that was owned by the very wealthy and fairly benevolent Godrej family. About twelve thousand people lived there and worked in the various Godrej factories. Most of them had the social status of *dalits*, or untouchables, and Mama fit into this category because of her work among them, her contact with human feces and other bodily excretions, and her habit of mopping floors and doing other menial work in her own living quarters. She earned a small stipend and was prohibited by Peace Corps rules from receiving money from her family back home.

The gardener for the owner's family was quite friendly to Mama and surreptitiously gave her vegetables and sometimes flowers. He told her that he had a son and a daughter, but his income permitted only the boy to be in school. Having no other way to repay him, she offered to teach the young girl how to read and write. She sent us a photograph of the child sitting with her on a big rock during one of the lessons. My sister Gloria Carter Spann collected the letters that my mother wrote from India, and they were later published in a book, *Away from Home: Letters to My Family*, that was quite popular after I became president. Later the publisher used the photograph on the rock as the cover of the paperback edition.

In 2006 Rosalynn and I led a group of Habitat for Humanity volunteers to build a hundred homes near Mumbai. We went a day early so we could visit Vikhroli, as guests of the Godrej family. They were very proud that we were visiting and had arranged for some of the people who had known Mama to meet us, including the doctor in whose clinic she worked and others who had been mentioned prominently in her letters. Almost a hundred people were assembled in a large room where Godrej consumer products were displayed, and we were all excited to meet each other. Toward the end of our scheduled time together, I noticed several copies of Mama's book lying around and I asked what had happened to the young girl in the photograph on the cover. Mr. Godrej responded that she was present and motioned for her to stand. She told us that she was president of the local university. Having spent my life in a society where there is little distinction between male and female students in educational opportunity, I still become emotional when I recount this vivid example of the advantages of education in the life of often excluded girls in the developing world.

Although I teach Bible lessons regularly, there are some parts of the New Testament and Hebrew text that I avoid, especially those that can be interpreted as promoting unnecessary violence or violating the basic standards of justice. There was a period in my life when I spent a lot of time studying the details of the Koran and how certain passages were interpreted by different believers. When I was president and American hostages were being held by Shiite Muslims in Iran, and during the war that followed between the Iranian Shiites and the Sunni Muslims in Iraq, I wanted to understand how I might use their religious beliefs to secure the release of the American diplomats and help bring peace to the region. I read through an English translation of their holy book, and the State Department and CIA provided some Islamic experts who conducted a series of sessions in the Oval Office to give me more detailed explanations. I came to understand more clearly how, in all major faiths, there is the essence of justice, peace, and compassion but that biased interpreters can twist their meaning.

As in Christian communities, the societal status of women varies widely within the Islamic world, and we in the West quite often fail to understand the high degree of political freedom and equality many of them enjoy. The Carter Center has monitored elections in Jordan, Egypt, Lebanon, Libya, Tunisia, Indonesia, Palestine, and Sudan, and we have assisted in preparation for elections in Bangladesh. In all these countries, as well as in Algeria, Iraq, Oman, Kuwait, Morocco, Syria, Mauritania, and Yemen and a number of others where Sharia law has a major influence, women and men have equal voting rights. There is no religious impediment to equal political rights for women ordained in the Koran.

This is a moment of truth, and people of faith working for human rights must be honest and acknowledge the role our own leadership plays for good or ill. We must speak out about the power of Islam to affect positive change in the lives of women, girls, and all people. We must take responsibility to spread this message. We should not wait for leaders to tell us, we should begin in childhood, at the grassroots, to educate our young about human rights, peace-building, and coexistence. By raising the voices of the voiceless, here we become a chorus and in sharing our ideas we support each other's efforts to advance the course of human rights around the world.

ALHAJI KHUZAIMA, EXECUTIVE SECRETARY,

ISLAMIC PEACE AND SECURITY COUNCIL IN GHANA

Saudi Arabia is a special case when dealing with the issue of gender equality. Saudi women have never been granted voting rights but may be permitted to vote in 2015, at least in municipal elections. There is a 150-member Consultative Assembly, or Shura, whose limited authority includes proposing laws for the king to consider, and it is encouraging to note that in 2013 he appointed thirty women as members. There is no doubt that Saudi Arabia plays the leadership role in the Islamic world, with its enormous wealth and its sovereign being the Custodian of the Two Holy Mosques. As president, I learned how valuable their assistance could be during some of my most challenging days. When Iran and Iraq went to war and their oil was removed from the world's supply, the Saudi king sent word to me that his kingdom would greatly increase production to help stabilize prices. There was an outpouring of condemnation from Arab leaders when I announced plans to go to Camp David with Israel and Egypt to negotiate a peace agreement, but I received quiet assurance from Saudi Arabia of their backing, and the king was the first to call me with congratulations when I left Egypt after announcing that a peace agreement was concluded.

These expressions of support were not made public because the Saudis strive to maintain harmony among the twenty-two members of the Arab League, and they deviate from majority opinion only with reluctance. Later, in 2002, Crown Prince (now King) Abdullah proposed an offer of peace with Israel based on recognition of the pre-1967 border between Israel and Palestine, which was supported by all Arab leaders and subsequently by the fifty-six Islamic nations (including Iran). When we launched the Carter Center program to eradicate Guinea worm in Asia and Africa, I went to Saudi Arabia to request a contribution from the king. One of my key points of persuasion was that this was a terrible affliction in Yemen and Pakistan and in African countries where many Muslims lived. He smiled and responded, "We will contribute $9 million, but want it to be used equally among people of all faiths."

On one of the visits that Rosalynn and I made to Riyadh, there had been an extraordinary rainfall of several inches just before our arrival, and pumps and tanker trucks were all over the city attempting to remove the standing water from low places. We were informed that King Fahd and his entourage were about 250 miles away in the desert, where he was meeting with tribal chieftains who had come to consult with him. The next day we boarded a helicopter for a flight to the encampment, and we were amazed at how the desert had blossomed with flowers, almost overnight. From the air we saw dozens of large tents arranged in a circle; connected to each one was a mobile home with attached electric generators and satellite antennae. A few miles over the sand dunes we could see a similar but smaller campsite that our pilot told us was for women.

Rosalynn was whisked away by Land Rover to join the women when we landed, while I joined the men. We lounged against large pillows on beautiful carpets spread on the leveled sand, and I spent a few hours discussing official business with the king. Then he granted my wish to observe the proceedings as a series of tribal chieftains came in to pay their respects, make their requests, and discuss matters of common interest. I spent two nights with them and enjoyed wonderful meals and entertainment. A number of sheep were roasted over charcoal flames, and we had a special treat of desert truffles that had been found after the rain. There were long and relaxed conversations around the campfires, with many vivid accounts of warfare and ribald stories about bedroom conquests and how the men choose the four wives permitted by their faith. Late each night we went into the luxurious air-conditioned mobile homes.

We knew about the strict dress codes for women, we had never seen women alone on the city streets, and we knew they were not permitted to drive an automobile or ride a bicycle. Each woman had an assigned male guardian, and only men could vote or hold public office. I was feeling somewhat sorry for Rosalynn, who I thought was stuck with a group of women whose faces were concealed and who were constrained by being treated as second-class citizens. Instead she had one of the most exciting and enjoyable visits of her life. The women bubbled over with pleasure as they extolled their enhanced status in Saudi society, with its special protection, plus freedom and privilege. They described their family vacations in more permissive Arab countries and special excursions to the French Riviera or the Swiss Alps. Her companions were, of course, mostly members of the royal family and wives and daughters of sheikhs and desert leaders, but we later learned that other women in the kingdom relish some customs that Westerners consider deprivations.

Changes are taking place. A majority of Saudi working women have a college education (compared to 16 percent of working men), and almost 60 percent of university students are women. However, about 78 percent of female university graduates are unemployed because of religious and cultural opposition. One manager of a grocery chain is challenging this policy and recently said, "We are promoting recruitment of Saudi women because they have a low level of attrition, a better attention to detail, a willingness to perform and productivity about twice that of Saudi men." Despite his best efforts, however, fewer than 5 percent of his employees are Saudi women. A Gallup poll in December 2007 indicated that the majority of women and men support women's rights to work and to drive. In October 2013 dozens of Saudi women in several cities protested the ban by openly driving; unlike in previous demonstrations, they were neither arrested nor punished.

The issue of polygamy comes up often in discussions with Muslims, and the key verse in the English translation of the Koran is 4:3: "If ye fear that ye shall not be able to deal justly with the orphans, marry women of your choice, two or three or four; but if ye fear that ye shall not be able to deal justly (with them), then only one, or that which your right hands possess, that will be more suitable, to prevent you from doing injustice." This scripture is interpreted in various ways in the Islamic world. As when the Bible was written many centuries earlier, husbands were all-powerful, and the desires and interests of women were considered to be relatively insignificant. I have discussed this issue with desert chiefs and other influential men in Arab countries, and most feel that the Koran permits them to have as many as four wives at a time. They usually emphasize that the intention of the Prophet was to enhance the status of women and orphans and that in modern days the willingness of the potential brides and the approval of existing wives are factors in determining the expansion of a family with additional marriages.

The Saudi ambassador in Washington, Prince Bandar, was especially helpful to me when I was president, and I invited him down to Georgia to observe our remarkable pointer and setter dogs in a quail hunt. We were on a large plantation in southwest Georgia, and after spending all day on horseback we enjoyed a typical southern supper and then gathered around an outdoor campfire with some friends of mine. They were quite interested in learning about hunting with falcons and plied the ambassador with many questions about his nation. One early query was, "How many wives do you have?" He replied, "I have only one, like many of my younger countrymen, but the Koran permits as many as four—at a time." He explained that a wife could be divorced just by the husband saying "I divorce thee" three times. Under further questioning, he commented that one of the senior princes had had fifty-six wives but had always retained his first wife as head of his household and never had more than four at a time. Each of those who were divorced was given a nice home and a stipend for life.

Islamic women at The Carter Center Human Rights Defenders Forum in 2013 insisted that the consequences for many women in multiple marriages could be devastating. They sometimes have little choice about who and when they marry, and because husbands have the religious and political authority to make all the decisions, wives suffer uncertainty about the future for themselves and their children.

The place of religion in our societies and in many states today, particularly in the Middle East, is the determining issue for our future. The issue of women's rights is the main battleground for determining the identity of a nation. If we protect women's rights, we get everything right. If we do not protect women's rights, everything will disintegrate. We have to settle the place of religion in our societies, and discuss it without fear of intimidation. When a society has not invested in protecting women against violence, religious leaders must stand up and demand that the state do so, with measures like street lights, police training, and prosecution of violators. The United Nations Human Rights Council has called upon all governments to prioritize such actions.

MONA RISHMAWI, OFFICE OF THE UNITED NATIONS
HIGH COMMISSIONER FOR HUMAN RIGHTS

The first extended overseas trip I made after leaving the White House was to China, to accept a long-standing invitation from Vice Premier Deng Xiaoping. In addition to visiting some of the most notable tourist sites with my family and a few friends, we also went to a number of rural areas where the first small and cautious experiments in free enterprise were becoming visible. Deng especially wanted me to witness one experiment, which was limited at that time just to farm families who did not live in a village or town. They were granted the right to grow their own private crops on as much as 15 percent of the land on communal farms and could have one small private commercial venture and retain the earnings. For instance, a family could repair bicycles, make horseshoes, produce iron nails, mold clay pots, or have as many as five chickens, pigs, goats, mink, or sheep, but only one of these enterprises at a time, and they could retain the income. The most impressive thing we observed was how proud and enthusiastic the cho-sen families were, and the apparent equality of treatment of women in managing the choice projects. This was something we had rarely seen in the developing world, before we began our later projects in Africa.

Rosalynn and I have visited China regularly since I left public office and have seen the improvements in the status of women. Statistics show that in education and employment they have equal opportunity, and their numbers in these areas are increasing rapidly. Marriage laws have removed sexual discrimination, and of the 2,987 members of the National People's Congress, 699 (23.4 percent) are women. There are now fourteen female cabinet officers, although women have never been represented among the top officials in the Central Committee. *Forbes* lists several Chinese women billionaires, and the Grant Thornton "International Business Report" states that half of senior management jobs in China are held by women, far above only 20 percent in the United States and a global average of 24 percent.

Nicholas Kristof, who lived for many years in China, writes in *Half the Sky* that "no country has made as much progress in improving the status of women as China has. Over the past one hundred years, it has become—at least in the cities—one of the best places to grow up female." This notable improvement is related directly to the role that women played in the Chinese Communist Party's long military struggle for power. A treatise entitled "Women in the Chinese Revolution (1921–1950)" states, "The battle for women's emancipation was closely tied up with the battle for social revolution in which they fought side by side with men." In 1950 the Marriage Law declared, "The arbitrary and compulsory feudal marriage system, which is based on the superiority of men over women, and which ignores the interests of children is abolished. The 'New Democratic Marriage System,' based on free choice of partners, on monogamy, on equal rights for both sexes and on protection of the lawful interests of women and children, shall be put into effect." It did not recognize a head of household and accorded equal status in the family to husband and wife.

There are exemplary guarantees of equal treatment in the laws of China and the ratification of the key international agreements, but the ancient traditions of gender discrimination are persistent, especially in remote rural areas. Officials explain that many women who held the higher-paying jobs in rural areas resigned and moved to the cities, leaving others behind, and claim that they are struggling to correct this disparity.

With a commitment to human rights as the foundation for our foreign policy when I was president, our nation abandoned its historic alliance with the dictatorships of Latin America. We observed with interest—but without involvement—the revolution in Nicaragua that was successful in overthrowing the regime of Anastasio Somoza Debayle in 1979. The revolutionary forces were headed by the Sandinistas but included a wide coalition of academics, business and professional leaders, and especially women. Women composed at least 30 percent of combatants in the revolutionary army, and their influence in shaping the new legal structure was unprecedented in the Western Hemisphere's independence struggles, with gender equality being a primary goal of the new government. One of the revolutionary leaders who came to visit me in the White House, along with the Sandinistas and others, was Violeta Chamorro, who was to be elected president of the nation in the first free and fair election, in 1990. Although she was timid in promoting women's issues during her time in office, the revolutionary commitment to women's rights has prevailed over the years. Nicaragua has by far the largest portion of women in Parliament in the Americas, at 40 percent. There have recently been some disturbing restrictions on the fairness and transparency of the electoral process and women's access to reproductive health services, but Nicaragua still stands out among all other countries in this hemisphere as foremost in gender equality, as measured by the World Economic Forum. In fact, only nine nations ranked higher than Nicaragua in this regard. Most European countries ranked lower, and the United States ranked only twenty-third.

It is not easy to determine or predict what historical events can help to equalize the status of women, but their enhanced status in China and Nicaragua indicates that military service contributes to this increased influence. Most Western nations admit women to serve on active duty in some capacity other than in the medical corps, and the United States has recently begun to assign women to combat roles, as do Canada, Denmark, Finland, Germany, Israel, Italy, New Zealand, Norway, Serbia, Sweden, Switzerland, and Taiwan. Their performance has been exemplary, and they have overcome the misgivings of many skeptics, including me. I have learned that my former doubts about the service of women were unjustified. Being "equal" in the military service helps to ensure that women will be more likely to demand and achieve the same status as men in political and economic matters.

8 | WOMEN AND THE CARTER CENTER

The Carter Center has confronted the issue of sexual discrimination and abuse of women through our work with families in remote communities in more than seventy developing nations, and we have seen how religious beliefs and violence have impacted their lives in patriarchal societies. Of even greater significance is what we have learned about the vital role that liberated women can play in correcting the most serious problems that plague their relatives and neighbors. Almost everywhere, we find that women are relegated to secondary positions of influence and authority within a community but almost always do most of the work and prove to be the key participants in any successful project. Whenever men are plagued with poverty, disease, or persecution, the women are suffering more. When there is a shortage of food or limited access to education, the men and boys have first priority. When there are few opportunities for jobs or desirable positions in any facet of life, they are rarely filled by women. When a civil conflict erupts, women are the primary victims of bombs and missiles, the displaced adults in charge of children, and the victims of rape. Beyond all this are the special biases that come from the distortion of religious beliefs and the imposition of discriminatory tribal customs that lead to honor killings, genital cutting, or child marriage.

Waging peace, fighting disease, and building hope are the major themes of The Carter Center, and one of our basic principles is not to duplicate what others are doing or to compete with them. If the U.S. government, World Health Organization, World Bank, or any university or nongovernmental organization is adequately addressing a problem, we don't get involved. We try to fill vacuums in the world, both in the projects we undertake and the regions in which we serve. Over the years we have mediated peace agreements, increased production of food grains in Africa, enhanced freedom and democracy by monitoring troubled elections, and defended human rights.

Somewhat to our surprise, we have been asked increasingly to concentrate our financial and personal resources in reducing the ravages of neglected tropical diseases, concentrating on trachoma, lymphatic filariasis (elephantiasis), onchocerciasis (river blindness), schistosomiasis, and dracunculiasis (Guinea worm). Under the direction of Dr. Don Hopkins, director of all our health programs, we also target malaria, since the same mosquito is the vector for filariasis. Although no longer found in developed countries, these diseases still afflict hundreds of millions of people in Africa and some regions in Latin America and Asia.

Early on we received criticism from well-meaning liberal friends that by saving lives in Africa we were contributing to the population explosion in the region and would be better engaged in improving education and agricultural production. I brought these suggestions to our health director at the time, Dr. William Foege, who was the former director of the Centers for Disease Control and had played the key role in eradicating smallpox. He produced official data to show me that the best way to reduce a high birthrate is for parents to be convinced that their children will live. There is a direct relation between reducing the infant mortality rate and a subsequent decrease in population growth. The logical explanation is that parents in poor regions depend on a certain number of surviving offspring to provide support in their older years; when child survival is doubtful, they produce the maximum number of children. It is also clear that a family's health is dependent on the knowledge of the mother about the advantages of good sanitation, proper diet, and other factors that can prevent or control prevalent diseases. Our primary health programs have been built on these premises for more than three decades.

Carter Center personnel or domestic trainees go into the most remote villages in the jungle or desert to teach people about their disease and what they can do to prevent it or ease the suffering. In doing this work, we have to become intimately involved in the daily lives of the people. If medicines, filter cloths, pesticides, or protective nets are required, we work with national health ministers, but we still retain control of the delivery system and let the local people do the work themselves. We give them full credit for success. Our focus on the most worthy projects is helped by the International Task Force for Disease Eradication (ITFDE), which is located at our Center and is the only organization of its kind. With participants from leading health organizations, the ITFDE regularly assesses all human illnesses to determine which might be targeted for elimination in a particular region or for global eradication.

Our most highly publicized struggle has been with dracunculiasis, or Guinea worm, and we are approaching our goal of having this be the second disease in history that is totally eradicated. This has been a massive effort lasting more than twenty-five years and involving direct intervention by our staff or trainees in more than 26,000 isolated villages in twenty countries. This long struggle has given us an unprecedented insight into the special role of women in some of the most destitute families on earth.

Guinea worm disease is caused by drinking contaminated water from a pond that fills during the rainy season and then becomes stagnant and slowly dries up during the rest of the year. Microscopic Guinea worm larvae in the water are consumed by tiny water fleas, which then are swallowed by people drinking the water. Inside a human's abdomen, the parasite larvae mate. Over about a year, the female matures and grows into a worm two to three feet long and begins emerging through the skin. The exit point is usually through the feet or legs but can be at any other part of the body.

A large sore develops around the emerging worm and is very painful, sometimes destroying muscle tissue so the aftereffect in a joint is similar to polio. There is almost unbearable pain for about thirty days, and the victim is incapacitated, unable to go to school or work in the field. There is no medical cure available, and the cause of the disease is usually unknown to villagers; many believe it must be a divine curse, derived from drinking goat's blood, the confluence of stars, or some other source. The only treatment for thousands of years has been performed by local religious leaders (or witch doctors), who wrap the emerging worm around a stick or other object about the size of a pencil and exert enough pressure to expedite the process by a few days. Care must be taken to pull out the entire worm, as any part remaining in the body will rot and become infected.

I first saw Guinea worm in a small village in Ghana, where about 350 of the 500 residents had worms coming out of their bodies. The villagers were assembled in an open space under large trees, except for about two dozen whose affliction was too great for them to walk or leave their hut. I noticed a lovely young woman on the edge of the crowd, holding a baby in her right arm, and after the ceremonies I went over to ask her the name of her child. But there was no baby; instead she was holding her right breast, which was almost a foot long and had a worm emerging from the nipple. Later I learned that a total of twelve worms emerged from different places in her body.

We had a wealthy man with us, and he paid for a well to be dug and a pump installed, so within a few weeks the pond was abandoned as a water source for the people. They have never had another case of Guinea worm in their village.

Like most other diseases in developing nations, Guinea worm especially affects the female members of a family. The first person expected to assist a sufferer is the mother or a girl child who must then be kept out of school. If people have learned the source of the disease, they naturally blame the women, who are almost invariably the ones who bring the water from the pond, often carrying five-gallon containers on their heads. To retrieve the water they walk into the pond, and if worms are emerging from their bodies thousands of eggs may be released to perpetuate the cycle. Fortunately it is also the women who assume responsibility for protecting their family and their village. For instance, more than 95 percent of our last remaining cases have been in South Sudan, where we are now concentrating our efforts. These final cases are very difficult to detect early and to control, and we have to expend an extraordinary effort to isolate people who contract the disease but also to monitor closely all the hundreds of villages where another case might reappear. Although in South Sudan there were 520 cases in 2012 and only 113 in 2013, we have retained about 120 people on our full-time payroll to perform these duties, most of them native to the area. They are assisted by more than ten thousand unpaid volunteers, all of them trained women who are trusted by other villagers.

Since the beginning of this effort in 1990, 131 women have served as our technical advisors, most of them holding a master's degree in public health. They have served in Sudan, South Sudan, Togo, Benin, Uganda, Ghana, Chad, Niger, Ethiopia, Nigeria, and other endemic countries. At our Carter Center headquarters in Atlanta, women have led our effort to gain publicity for the program and to secure funding to cover its costs. All these women have interacted with each other and gained a special insight into the massive challenges and how to overcome them. Among the six thousand women who conducted the extensive survey to detect new cases in Ghana, one leader expressed the feeling of many of her fellow workers, most of them previously excluded from leading such efforts: "It's about time they involved us. We're the only ones who know how things work anyway."

The final stages of eliminating Guinea worm disease from Nigeria were headed by the country's former president General Yakubu Gowon. When excluded from a decision about how to treat a village pond in Nigeria, a group of women with newfound self-confidence confronted him and stopped the process because approval had been obtained only from the male village leaders. Gowon quickly corrected his mistake.

In the beginning one of our biggest obstacles was to educate people in all the small and isolated communities about this ancient blight and how to eliminate it. Without television or radio service and when communities five miles apart speak different languages and only a few men are just partially literate, we had to devise a completely new form of communication. We finally resorted to cartoons: simple drawings of women dipping water from a pond and drinking it. Those who were shown using a filter were all right, but the others had worms coming out of their body. Women wrote original plays and songs to explain the process and printed the colored cartoons onto cloth, which was used to make dresses and shirts for other members of their family. I was proud when they gave me one of the shirts on a visit with them.

Some of the people had never seen a picture or photograph before, and this would occasionally cause problems. One group of Peace Corps volunteers in a remote area of Niger made some of the drawings, showing the women standing in the knee-deep pond. When the villagers first saw the cartoon, a chorus of voices cried, "I'd rather have Guinea worm than no feet!"

Of all the "neglected" diseases on which The Carter Center has focused its efforts to control or eradicate, blinding trachoma is the only one twice as common in women as in men. It also is the only one of these diseases that I knew when I was a child. We depended on horses and mules to pull our plows and vehicles and raised cattle, sheep, hogs, goats, geese, ducks, and chickens to provide food for our family and surplus meat, eggs, and milk to sell for additional income. Our barn lot was usually ankle deep in manure and rainwater, and most of what my sisters and I swept from our yard with brush brooms was droppings from the free-roaming fowl. We were always surrounded by swarms of houseflies, even inside our home, despite screens on our doors and windows, and they were especially attracted to children's eyes as they sought moisture and sustenance. Flies carry filth that causes infection, and I was almost constantly afflicted with sore eyes that my mother would treat to prevent development into the more serious trachoma. Some of our neighbors were not so fortunate. The advanced stage causes the upper eyelids to turn inward, slashing the cornea with every blink and causing blindness. I was reminded of this in more recent years when we visited the villages and homes of Dinka and Masai families in Kenya, Sudan, and other African countries. From a distance the children appear to be wearing eyeglasses; nearby, it is seen to be a ring of flies encircling their eyeballs, searching for moisture.

Except for cataracts, trachoma is the most prevalent cause of blindness, still afflicting tens of millions of the world's poorest people. The Carter Center combats trachoma in almost a dozen countries in Africa, having begun this effort in Ghana in 1998. There is a comprehensive treatment program recommended by the World Health Organization that uses the acronym SAFE: surgery, antibiotics, face washing, and environment. We have eliminated blinding trachoma in several countries, and our major challenge is now in Ethiopia, where we have concentrated our efforts for many years. In 2000 the Pfizer pharmaceutical company agreed to my request for a free supply of azithromycin (Zithromax), which is the best antibiotic for treating trachoma. In November 2013 we administered our one-hundred-millionth dose. We have taught several thousand health workers, mostly women, to perform eyelid surgeries, a simple process with adequate training, and provided them with the necessary sterile instruments. They now perform about 40 percent of these operations in the world. We also marshaled schoolteachers and parents in the endemic areas to encourage children to wash their face, which they had never thought of doing before.

In correcting the problem in a community, women are the agents for change in health education, responsible for cleanliness in the home, taking care of laundry, and educating their children in hygienic behavior. In treating trachoma and other diseases on a broad scale, the Ministry of Health in Ethiopia has learned that women enjoy a greater level of trust from heads of households and better access to neighbors' homes than men. We have been able to train 6,500 health extension workers in the Amhara region, and all are women. They lead teams that now distribute up to 20 million doses of Zithromax each year to treat infected eyes. In recent months the ministry has implemented a new all-volunteer corps of female health workers, called the 1 to 5 Health Development Army because they select one-fifth of the families and train them to minister to four others. Early in 2013 we mobilized over twenty thousand of these volunteers and saw the population coverage with Zithromax increase to almost 93 percent. Our health experts attribute this success to the Health Development Army having a personal and close relationship with their neighbors and therefore noticing if specific individuals are missing treatments.

Our specialists in trachoma observed that one new volunteer to become an "eye surgeon" had a scar on her eyelids. She explained that her advanced trachoma infection had been corrected by surgery performed by one of her trained neighbors. Her life was changed; instead of having a disabling condition leading to misery, poverty, and total blindness, she became an active health promoter for her community. She was proud yet tearful when she told her full story.

Having dealt with surgery, antibiotics, and face washing, (S-A-F), this left the problem of the environment (E): the ubiquitous flies that breed and feed on a constant supply of human and animal excrement and carry infection from one person to another. Surprisingly, it was a "women's liberation movement" that gave us a major breakthrough in solving this problem. I remembered that we had had an outdoor privy behind our house (the only one on the farm) and that we had covered our home site with strong doses of powdered or liquid DDT, a poison that controlled flies, mosquitoes, and other insects. This was a key factor in ridding ourselves of both trachoma and malaria. (It was later learned that DDT was also eliminating butterflies and many birds, especially those species like hawks and other raptors that consumed bodies within which the long-lasting pesticide had accumulated, so the outdoor use of DDT is now prohibited throughout the world.) We knew that in Ethiopia and other regions in Africa many men simply step behind a bush to defecate and are often seen urinating alongside roads and highways, but we learned that it was absolutely taboo for a woman to be seen relieving herself. The most convenient recourse for themselves and their daughters was to find a concealed place in or around the family home. Working with local people, we taught them how to build latrines as a means to improve the environment by reducing the population of flies. It is a very simple design that consists of a hole in the ground, some way to prevent the hole from caving in while a person stands or squats over it, and an enclosure of brush or cloth for privacy. If the family provides the labor, the financial cost is only about a dollar. We were hoping for a few thousand latrines to be built during the first year, but the word spread from village to village as Ethiopian housewives adopted this as a practical move toward liberation, and the total number of latrines built that year was 86,500! By the end of 2012 we had seen 2.9 million latrines built as more wives and mothers demanded this beneficial addition to their freedom and health. I am proud of my growing reputation as the world's most preeminent sponsor of latrines.

This somewhat humorous account illustrates that despite their inferior social status, these women were strong and even dominant, deeply involved in all aspects of improving health care, and extremely effective in solving their own problems, with associated benefits to their entire community.

In fact, though formerly excluded from positions of leadership or responsibility, dedicated and competent women have been the key to our success in every health project. We responded to a request from the prime minister of Ethiopia in 1992 to train health workers for the general population of about 82 million. He stipulated that they would not be permitted to leave Ethiopia in the process, as he was concerned that they would not return after graduation. We developed a curriculum for each of the diseases and health problems they faced (about seventy) and used local university campuses for classes. The final result after ten years was 7,000 graduates who have the capability of a physician's assistant or registered nurse, plus 27,000 with training equivalent to a licensed practical nurse. This was enough to provide a female health worker for every 2,400 citizens, deployed as evenly as possible throughout the country.

A significant revelation of these programs has been that people who live with poverty and disease, with little self-respect or hope for a better future, can have their lives and attitudes transformed by tangible success brought about by their own efforts. They have demonstrated vividly that, despite their devastating poverty, they are just as intelligent, just as ambitious, just as hardworking as people with much greater economic and educational resources. Like people everywhere, they seek to secure physical, emotional, and spiritual health for their families and their communities. And it is most often the women who lead in these initiatives.

In 1986 we launched a program in Africa to increase the production of basic food grains, mostly maize (corn), wheat, rice, sorghum, and millet. Our partners were a Japanese philanthropist, Ryoichi Sasakawa, and Dr. Norman Borlaug, who had been awarded the Nobel Prize for Peace in 1970 for inaugurating the "green revolution" in India and Pakistan. We named the program Global 2000 and worked only with subsistence farmers who usually had no more than a hectare (about two acres) of land on which the entire family depended for food and, in good years, some surplus to sell for cash income. Utilizing my own experience as a full-time farmer for seventeen years and especially the scientific and practical advice from Dr. Borlaug, we were able to double or triple production for those who used good seed, planted in rows, controlled the weeds, harvested at the right time, and had storage facilities that minimized damage from moisture, insects, and rodents. Eventually 8 million families in fifteen nations completed our program, and we gave awards to the most outstanding farmers in each nation.

One memorable event occurred when Rosalynn and I went to Zimbabwe to present this award to a farmer who lived about 125 miles from Harare, the capital. When we arrived in the village we found the entire population of the area assembled in the town square, a bare spot surrounded by homes and a few trees. Local officials were assembled under a large tree, and we noticed one man standing with them, erect and nervous, wearing a dusty black suit and a flowery tie. He was introduced to us as the Global 2000 Outstanding Farmer, and we gave him a plaque and a financial award.

We had made prior arrangements to eat lunch in his home, where he was quite loquacious and kept us amused with anecdotes about his parents, his early life, and some of his adult exploits. After we finished our meal, carefully served by his very quiet wife, I suggested that we visit his crops. He objected strenuously—about the path being rough, getting our clothes dirty, and the heat. I insisted, pointing out that we lived in South Georgia and had spent many years on the farm. Furthermore I had worn my khaki trousers and work boots, so I didn't mind getting dirty. He finally yielded, and we walked down the hill to a beautiful stand of maize. I was impressed and asked him a series of questions involving the variety he planted, spacing in the row, growing season, fertilizer used, and expected harvest date. He did not know how to respond to any of the questions, and in every case he turned to his wife for the answer. Very shyly, she explained the entire process she had followed in actually becoming the most Outstanding Farmer in Zimbabwe. We learned that her husband just cared for the cattle and collected the money when his wife's good crops were sold.

Although our Center is not involved directly in microloans, we have observed women's groups initiate their own programs. Often for the first time, these loans gave the recipients some financial independence from their husbands for purchasing personal items for themselves and their children. Using profits from producing or processing grain or making soap or handmade products, women started local banks that made small loans to others, and the custom spread widely. Since women are the primary farmers in many areas of Africa, it became increasingly common to see them directly managing the harvest, storage, and even marketing of grain. Rosalynn and I visited one of our agricultural sites in Togo as the maize crop was being brought in to a central marketplace, and all the weighing, accounting, assignment to storage bins, and disbursements were being conducted by women. It was like a combined farmers' market and bank. They had devised a computer system using a row of nails, all of the same height, and had stacks of coins with perforated centers; exactly ten coins would fit on a nail, so the decimal system was automatically utilized as tabulation proceeded. The women were also grinding corn into meal and selling it along with handicraft items, including exquisite pottery. We still have some of the pots on our back porch.

If the [developing] world was a molecule put under a powerful microscope, we would see a complex web of barriers that keep women from fully realizing their inherent human rights and living in dignity. Strands of this web include barriers to securing property rights; pursuing an education and earning a decent living at fair wages; making decisions about love, sex, and marriage; controlling one's reproduction; and obtaining health care. We would also see the invisible DNA that keeps this web intact: a sense of powerlessness, enforced by social coercion, rigid gender roles, homophobia, violence, and rape. Finally, we also would see that only the women

who face these barriers can push them aside, change their
own lives, and transform the societies in which they live. It is
our obligation to support them.

RUTH MESSINGER, PRESIDENT,

AMERICAN JEWISH WORLD SERVICE

In 1978 I was the first American president to visit Sub-Saharan Africa, and it was not incidental that one of my destinations was Liberia. That nation's government had been founded in the early nineteenth
century by freed American slaves, freeborn blacks from the United
States, and others who were liberated from European ships that were
taking them to the New World to be sold. I had known Liberia's president, William Tolbert, when he was the leader of the Baptist World
Alliance. Two years after my visit, President Tolbert and all his cabinet were assassinated and the country was afflicted with civil strife,
until a peace agreement was finally reached in 1995. During that time
Rosalynn and I and other representatives of The Carter Center made
many visits to the capital, Monrovia, and to the 95 percent of the country that was under the control of various warlords. We monitored the
process when an election could be orchestrated, and the strongest war-
lord, Charles Taylor, was elected in 1997, primarily because many voters feared that civil war would again erupt if he was defeated. He was
a despotic and oppressive ruler who promoted warfare in neighboring
countries. After he was overthrown and forced into exile by opposition
headed by a phalanx of women, in 2005 we monitored another free and
fair election that was won by Ellen Johnson Sirleaf, the first woman
to be elected president in Africa. (Taylor was convicted of war crimes
by the Special Court for Sierra Leone and sentenced to fifty years of
imprisonment.)

The vast region of Liberia formerly controlled by warlords had become isolated from the central government and was basically lawless.
The new president asked us to help her minister of justice evolve a legal
system in the rural areas that would protect human rights, be under-

standable to the populace, and make the citizens and their local political leaders feel that they shared the responsibility of maintaining the laws. As our programs evolved, it became increasingly apparent that their most powerful impact was on women, who had little protection under previous laws and tribal customs.

We worked to inform the people, for the first time, that rape was a crime and that perpetrators could be punished, that women could own property, that a wife could inherit her deceased husband's estate, that both parents had claims on their children, that there was a minimum legal age of marriage, that female genital cutting was not mandatory, and that a dowry was a gift and did not have to be returned if a marriage broke up. Most of this was new to them, of course, and there was opposition in a society where women had never demanded nor been granted these rights.

Using the carefully chosen slogan "Empower Men and Women Together," we began to frame issues of gender equality and violence with community dramas, training of traditional leaders, and use of radio broadcasts. For the first time women were encouraged to participate equally in the performances, discussions on the radio, and face-to-face debates. The most intriguing, and sometimes disturbing, subject for the traditional chiefs was the relationship between customary and statutory laws. With support from the minister of justice and the local leaders, we worked with the Catholic Justice and Peace Commission to establish forty-seven community justice advisors (CJAs), of which seventeen are women. They now operate in the five largest counties and have opened almost seven thousand cases, 71 percent of which have been resolved. About 40 percent of the cases involved domestic disputes, 33 percent related to financial and property claims, and 15 percent were criminal cases. The largest group that uses the CJAs are young women, and the largest single case category is child abandonment. Through March 2013 cases had been initiated by 2,694 men and 2,773 women. An independent study by Oxford University of four hundred representative cases reported an improvement in legal knowledge, a reduction in bribery, and an increase in community acceptance of the law, producing "large socioeconomic benefits . . . not by bringing the rural poor into the formal domain of magistrates' courts, government offices, and police stations, but by bringing the formal law into the organizational forms of the custom, through low-cost third-party mediation and advocacy."

Even more significant was a statement by Ella Musu Coleman, a leader of the National Traditional Council of Liberia: "The Carter Center doesn't tell us what to do. They help us understand what the law is, and why some of our traditions are not correct. We decide amongst ourselves if we want to get rid of certain practices." Both she and Chief Zanzan Karwar, the chairman of Liberia's National Traditional Council, attended the 2013 Human Rights Defenders Forum at The Carter Center and expressed strong support for the seminal improvements that have been made in the lives of their people.

Deliberately we did not set out to address the issue of female genital cutting (FGC), which is deeply entrenched and a subject not normally discussed publicly. Liberia is one of the African countries where no laws have been adopted to curtail the practice. However, it has been debated among women leaders and in the government and international NGOs, who have faced opposition to its abolition from local men and women. A partner of The Carter Center, Mama Tumah, the head female *zoe* (traditional leader), has been open to new ideas, and in her own village she has removed the sacred grove involved in FGC ceremonies. Most recently she convened a group of women *zoes* from all of Liberia's fifteen counties to discuss the issue among themselves. The closing ceremony was attended by four female government ministers.

It is clear that more equal female involvement in community affairs is beneficial to *all* citizens but is best achieved by letting the local people—both men and women—make their own decisions. The experiences of The Carter Center and our African coworkers show that there are ways to encourage these changes in social norms, but this work will require a lot of patience and a tremendous amount of humility and mutual respect.

An issue that The Carter Center has addressed on a global basis for fifteen years is access to information. Headed by legal expert Laura Neuman, this program seeks to encourage all nations to provide citizens with the ability to know what their governments are doing by passing laws that reveal how decisions are made, how public funds are spent, the terms of contracts for mining and timber harvesting, and the accurate and timely promulgation of voter lists and the results of elections. Access to such information is one of our fundamental human rights, enshrined in Article 19 of the Universal Declaration of Human Rights, which states, "Everyone has the right to . . . seek, receive and impart information." This same language is repeated in the International Covenant on Civil and Political Rights, the American Convention on Human Rights, and the European Convention on Human Rights. I have attended regional conferences on this subject in Ghana, Peru, Jamaica, Costa Rica, and China and an international forum in Atlanta. Having this right to information increases citizens' confidence in their leaders, makes public administration more efficient and effective, guarantees that natural resources will be better utilized, and increases confidence of potential investors. It also promotes the desire of citizens to become involved in elections and other public affairs.

Even in countries that have legal guarantees of these rights, one tragic finding is that the marginalized, poverty-stricken, least educated people are mostly excluded from access to fundamental information. This is especially true for women. As explained in the UN Millennium Development Goals report of 2011, women perform 66 percent of all the work but continue to form the largest bloc of the world's poor, an estimated 70 percent of the 1.3 billion people living in poverty. Girls are less likely than boys to attend primary school, and more of them have to leave school because of poverty or a need to work. This trend accelerates for secondary education. The *Global Education Digest* of 2012 concludes that this has led to approximately 66 percent of illiterate persons being women. Their relative poverty, illiteracy, lack of mobility, and much smaller proportion of membership in parliaments make clear that women suffer most from lack of information—and from corruption. A study conducted by the United Nations Development Program and UN Women found that " 'petty' or 'retail' corruption" (when basic public services are sold) affects poor women in particular and that "women and girls are often asked to pay bribes in the form of sexual favors." In a vicious circle, lack of access to public officials leaves women vulnerable to corruption, but their low income diminishes their ability to pay bribes, further restricting their access to basic services. In addition, their need to take care of their family often prevents women from having time to seek protection from corruption.

We have come to the conclusion that many of the other abuses of women and girls (slavery, genital cutting, child marriage, rape) can be reduced only if women have more access to information about the international, national, and local agencies that are responsible for publicizing and ending these abuses. It is difficult for women and their defenders to demand their legitimate rights if they don't know what they deserve under their own nation's laws. We are conducting studies in Liberia and Guatemala to ascertain how well international standards are being met. Liberia is making good progress under the leadership of President Johnson Sirleaf, but Guatemala is greatly lacking in transparency.

Top Guatemalan officials have agreed to cooperate with our program, since official reports of rape and sexual assault increased by 34 percent from 2008 to 2011, and an estimated 50 percent of women have suffered from domestic violence. During the first six months of 2013 more women were murdered in Guatemala than in any other complete year, and only one in ten cases of violence against women results in punishment of the offender. In our assessments so far, 75 percent of interviewees claim that women receive less public information than men; this is due to their timidity about asking for information, fear of retribution, lack of awareness about availability of information, and lack of mobility. For instance, 90 percent of those entering the birth registry department and 80 percent entering the business registry office during our observation period in early 2013 were men, and men received interviews and help from public officials much faster than women, who were largely ignored.

These are some of the basic questions we are asking in our studies in Liberia and Guatemala:

> *Education:* Are women able to access information on educational policies, school budgets, curricula, nutritional programs, and scholarships?
>
> *Land ownership:* Are women able to access information on land policy, their rights to own or inherit land, and do they have access to land titles?
>
> *Starting a business:* Do women have access to information about obtaining a business license, procedures for starting and sustaining a small business, access to loans, laws regarding taxation, imports, or marketing?
>
> *Farming:* Do women have access to information about prices for land rent, seed, fertilizer, irrigation water, or about market prices at harvest time?

When these surveys are complete, we will convene meetings of international and regional groups to consider how best to improve access to information for women as a way to reduce existing impediments to their equal treatment as citizens.

9 | LEARNING FROM HUMAN RIGHTS HEROES

Our continuing experiences in different countries and with other organizations have been correlated with efforts to promote human rights more specifically. We have had Human Rights Defenders Forums at The Carter Center for many years with participants from the United Nations and about a dozen of the most prominent human rights organizations to discuss urgent issues. Our custom has been to invite about forty of the most notable human rights heroes from nations with oppressive regimes and then to use our best efforts to obtain permission for them to join us. My personal intercessions are sometimes inadequate, but just focusing our attention on them provides some protection even if they are not permitted to leave their country. Those who are able to attend these conferences of human rights defenders can learn from each other about tactics, and they derive encouragement from being together for frank and unrestrained discussions of the challenges they face. We have been successful each year in arranging a roundtable interview on CNN in Atlanta and for some of the key participants to go to Washington for meetings with representatives from the U.S. Congress and leaders from the executive branch.

Over the years human rights activists have increasingly emphasized that the example set by the United States was having enormous influence on whether their own governments, often with less commitment and experience with the rule of law and protection of human rights, would follow in America's footsteps. For example, America's "war on terror" gave governments from countries like Kenya, Pakistan, Egypt, and Nigeria more latitude to violate prohibitions against torture and indefinite detention without due process in a vague and open-ended pursuit of national security. We decided to convene a session in 2003 titled "Reinforcing the Frontlines of Freedom: Protecting Human Rights in the Context of the War on Terror." News of the establishment of the Guantánamo Bay detention facility for the purpose of detaining indefinitely people suspected of terrorism, along with what the majority of the world considered an illegal aggressive war against Iraq, led many to believe it was necessary to launch a movement for renewed commitment to the provisions of international law and the Universal Declaration of Human Rights.

The forum issued the "Atlanta Declaration," which called on all governments to align national security policies with human rights principles such as the absolute prohibition of torture, access to due process of law, fair trials for any person deprived of liberty, and adherence to the Geneva Conventions and other international humanitarian laws. I wrote a book, *Our Endangered Values*, about this set of challenges and delivered a speech at the Democratic National Convention in 2004 that focused on the urgent task of restoring America's position as a champion of human rights and democratic ideals. In our forums we included women activists, as the Center considers women's rights issues a key component of all our programs rather than a separate concern. Women suffer most during and after war and have a central role to play in advancing peace and preventing the radicalization of young people during times of conflict.

During the 2003 forum, one of Afghanistan's greatest leaders, Dr. Sima Samar, the nation's first female doctor and government minister, expressed her view that by waging war "in the name of democracy and human and women's rights," the international coalition might embolden the extremists. She insisted that progress was possible only through supporting credible and legitimate Afghan democratic forces and initiatives and that an excessive military approach would undermine these objectives. Over the next several years, Dr. Samar expressed growing alarm at the increase in civilian deaths, intrusive and deadly night raids, assassination by drones, and indefinite detention of Afghans in facilities that mirrored conditions at Bagram prison or Guantánamo Bay. Sadly many of the same issues we discussed in 2003 persist. Later I wrote an op-ed for the *New York Times* in which I described in detail how the United States was currently violating at least ten of the thirty articles of the Universal Declaration of Human Rights.

In 2007 we convened our Human Rights Defenders Forum on the theme of "Faith and Freedom," in which we explored how religious leaders and communities can become stronger in their advocacy of human rights. We found reluctance among some secular human rights organizations to examine intersections with religion. The history of oppression on religious grounds is well known and is a matter of sensitivity among advocates who rely on global agreements that are seen as transcending religion, such as the Universal Declaration of Human Rights. We also encountered resistance among some religious persons and leaders because of their perception that the human rights concept focuses on the individual instead of collective well-being. We also were quietly informed that many religious people and institutions automatically associate the human rights framework with the promotion of homosexual and abortion rights, so they were reluctant to become too closely associated with the movement.

Despite these impediments, the conference was very successful, and we began exploring ways that religion can be a powerful force for equality and universal human dignity. This exploration led us to the conclusion that there is no greater challenge than the full embrace of women's equal rights by religious leaders, institutions, and believers alike. We found also that we could hardly address the deprivations of women's rights without also confronting an even larger challenge posed by a growing acceptance of violence. These two forums, held ten years apart, brought us to the same conclusion: that a new commitment to universal human rights and to end unnecessary violence is desperately needed if humanity is to escape the cycle of war, poverty, and oppression.

During this series of forums and our other work at The Carter Center, we became increasingly aware that one of the most crucial issues is the pervasive violation of the rights of women and girls, and in 2011 this was the subject of our assembly. Many of the participants were from Islamic countries, and they recommended that we move one of our subsequent venues to a predominantly Muslim community.

I wanted to understand more fully the attitude of internationally admired and prominent men toward women in an Islamic society, and that led me to the Egyptian Naguib Mahfouz, the 1988 Nobel Laureate in literature. I remembered that when Anwar Sadat was widely condemned throughout the Islamic world after signing the peace treaty with Israel in 1979, Mahfouz was a prominent defender of Sadat's decision. Like Sadat, Mahfouz was attacked by an assassin and severely wounded in 1994; he died twelve years later. I obtained his book *Life's Wisdom from the Works of the Nobel Laureate*, which was described by the editor as a "distilled collection of quotations from this great author's works." I found that they provided a fascinating if disturbing array of comments from the perspective of a man I knew as a progressive and thoughtful Islamic intellectual:

> Girls today no longer have the ability to get along with people. Where are the ladies of yesteryear?
>
> Only men can ruin women, and not every man is capable of being a guardian for them.
>
> Marriage is the ultimate surrender in life's losing battle.
>
> The virtue of marriage is that it takes care of one's lust and so purifies the body.
>
> Marriage is just a big deception. After a few months as tasty as olive oil, your bride turns into a dose of castor oil.

Women's lack of ideology or philosophy proves that ideology and philosophy hinder real, vital activity. A woman is only concerned with creation and all things connected, she is a beautiful creator, and creation is the center of her life. All other activities are of man's making and are necessary for domination, not creation!

Just as one can find a deviant housewife, there's an honorable working woman.

The love of a woman is like political theater: there is no doubt about the loftiness of its goal, but you wonder about the integrity of it.

A woman without children is like wine without the power to intoxicate, like a rose without scent, or like worship without strong faith behind it.

I was relieved to read this lonely quotation toward the end of this presentation of his work:

Women's liberation is not limited to equal rights and duties: it also implies their full participation in the political and economic as well as social and cultural spheres.

These comments by a world-renowned Islamic scholar indicate that even within a modern and ostensibly secular society there is a tendency to ridicule and derogate women and their role in the family and the general society.

Equality between women and men in the Quran is clear. But I have a suggestion for men: they need to support women in the issue of equality by sometimes just being silent.

SHEIKH OMAR AHMED TIJANI NIASS,

SPIRITUAL LEADER OF THE TIJANI SUFI ORDER OF ISLAM

We monitored very closely the overthrow of President Hosni Mubarak of Egypt in 2011 in a popular uprising, and our Center closely witnessed the subsequent elections for a parliament, a president, and the formulation of a new constitution. I had first met Dr. Mohamed Morsi in 2011 when he was head of the engineering department at Zagazig University near Cairo. Neither of us had any idea that he would be the first democratically elected president. During the subsequent months he assured me that the terms of the Egypt-Israel peace treaty would be honored and that any modifications desired by the Egyptians would be negotiated peacefully with Israel. Another issue on which we reached agreement was the rights of women. Dr. Morsi told me that he was working with a panel established by the grand imam of Al-Azhar on a statement that would spell out policies on the status of women and girls in an Islamic society. The grand imam was president of Al-Azhar University, which had 120,000 students, and was the spiritual leader of Sunni Muslims.

I met with Grand Imam Ahmed el-Tayeb on my subsequent visits to Egypt and found him to be quite moderate concerning the basic freedoms of society and dedicated to formulating a public statement concerning the gender issue. After our private discussions he always invited about a dozen leaders of the various Christian denominations in Cairo for more broad-ranging topics. The Christian leaders were not involved in drafting the Al-Azhar statement on the rights of women but likely would be guided by the stated policies of Muslims, who comprise 90 percent of the nation's population. Because of the sensitivity of women's rights in many Islamic countries and because of promised support by President Morsi, the grand imam, and the pope of the Coptic Church, we made plans to hold our annual Human Rights Defenders Forum in Egypt in June 2013 and were assured by government authorities of their approval and support.

The Egyptian military establishment seemed to grant authority to the new government, but they had ruled Egypt for almost sixty years and all the members of the Supreme Court had been appointed by former president Mubarak. These justices declared the carefully moni-tored and successful election of parliamentary members to be invalid, and the police force was strangely ineffective in maintaining order on the streets. Very little foreign aid flowed into Egypt except for military purposes. Under these circumstances, President Morsi proved an inef-fective leader and turned increasingly to his own Muslim Brotherhood associates for support and guidance. After massive popular demon-strations by opposition forces Morsi was overthrown and imprisoned by military coup in July 2013, with total authority reverting to the military.

Meanwhile, the threat of street demonstrations had required us to change the location of our Human Rights Defenders Forum from Cairo to The Carter Center. We contacted everyone on our guest list and invited them to come to Atlanta, and almost all of them were able to do so. The subject was "Mobilizing Faith for Women," and the world's major religions and geographical regions were represented. The participants included religious leaders who were Protestant, Catholic, and Coptic Christians, Sunni, Shia, and Sufi Muslims, conservative and progressive Jews, Baha'i, tribal traditionalists, and other activists who focused the work of their organizations on rape, slavery, child marriage, genital cutting, economic and social deprivation, and other sexual abuses.

Before our session I read *Half the Sky*, a remarkable book by Nicho-las Kristof and his wife, Sheryl WuDunn, its title derived from a state-ment by Chairman Mao Zedong: "Women hold up half the sky." The authors interviewed hundreds of courageous women and girls who were suffering from persecution because of their gender and who were will-ing to describe their plight. Often they were struggling, at the risk of death, for their human rights. Nick has traveled with us at times to observe our Center's efforts to promote peace and freedom and to con-trol the many diseases that take their heaviest toll among women and children. He and Sheryl have done as much to promote women's rights as anyone I know.

We learned at our conference that it is easier for Christians to deviate from certain Bible scriptures with which they disagree or consider not applicable to modern society than for Muslims to disregard similar passages in the Koran. However, in both Christian and Islamic societies, secular customs vary widely in the treatment of women.

From the participants in our conference we derived as much information as possible about different religions and geographical areas concerning the status of women and girls. The delegates from Egypt represented the grand imam, the Coptic pope, the Library of Alexandria, and women activists. Although the final version of the Al-Azhar Declaration on Women's Rights was not issued because of the political turmoil, we were given a working draft that was quite encouraging. A quote from the preamble sets the tone:

> The Islamic point of view regarding the position of women, their rights and duties towards themselves, their families and their societies, stems from the values which represent legal principles and general rules out of which rulings and arrangements directed to both men and women are born. These represent an equal and comprehensive view of mankind of both genders, with the aim of achieving happiness and stability to the individual, the family and society.
>
> . . . Contemporary women's positions need to be safeguarded, hence the need for this document. For proper positioning represents the most important element of reforming society and purifying it from wrong practices as well as recent social customs that are not based on clear textual evidence or proper jurisprudence, and which bring injustice and pain to men and women, though their toll falls more heavily on women.

After a reminder that "the Council of Senior Religious Scholars launches this document free of any outside pressures or transient political leanings," there is this statement:

It comes from a perspective that respects Islamic heritage. Both its principles and branches work to maintain and renovate this heritage according to its own values and logic, while reminding all that these values and rulings represent a leap in the liberation of women in classical Islamic times, on a world scale, when Arab traditions in this field were backward and religious thinking in the medieval European period questioned whether a woman was human or something else! These values and practical principles were implemented in the golden age of Islamic civilization; thus the Muslim woman enjoyed financial independence a thousand years before her peers in the West, and her right to inheritance, suitable employment and unlimited education. In fact, many Imams studied with renowned women scholars themselves. Similarly a woman enjoyed the right to choose a husband, look after the affairs of her family, demand *khul* (annulment of marriage) or separation in the event of damage or need. This is the reason why Muslim societies did not witness familial struggles or women's social revolutions that other societies suffered from.

I have found the grand imam to be remarkably immune to "transient political leanings" and have high expectations for a reasonable and spiritually inspired text when the final document is published. Its balanced position on the rights of Muslim men and women will have a beneficial effect on those spiritual and secular leaders who are seeking to apply the teachings of the Koran in modern times. However, although the grand imam is the spiritual leader of more than 80 percent of all Muslims, political leaders in predominantly Islamic nations are not bound by his statements or declarations on societal relationships.

While Egyptian women are ready to seek change in society, the culture is still not ready to view them as equals. We must

change this by challenging students and religious leaders to re-think and re-read the Koran for gender justice. As a Muslim, I believe that Islam came with a feminist revolution in Arabia. But what we have right now is a very patriarchal, traditional understanding of Islam, and this understanding is widespread. Religious leaders must support women's rights and gender justice in Egypt by leading their followers back to the true essence of religion: the equality and democratic nature at the heart of Islam. Despite these restraints, women are active in the streets of Egypt, in Upper Egypt in the rural areas. They are defending their voices to be heard, and they reject marginalization.

DR. RIHAM BAHI, SCHOLAR OF ISLAMIC AND
SECULAR FEMINISM AND ASSOCIATE PROFESSOR AT
THE AMERICAN UNIVERSITY OF CAIRO

When Rosalynn and I founded The Carter Center in 1982 we had an office on the campus of Emory University. I was teaching and giving lectures regularly, planning and raising funds for a presidential library, and receiving some visitors who sought appointments with me to discuss issues left over from my White House years. One of these requests came from a Coptic priest in America, and I was surprised when about two dozen priests crowded into my office, all in their sober black robes and hoods. They explained that their pope, Shenouda III, was under house arrest in a desert monastery in Egypt and that the worldwide functions of their faith were severely handicapped because all official actions were legitimate only if the directives were from their cathedral, which he was forbidden to visit.

I promised to help and soon learned that the detention order was supported by President Mubarak. I had known him well as the hand-picked vice president and personal emissary of President Sadat. I called Mubarak and told him that I was speaking for the Copts as a fellow Christian. The pope was released from captivity in January 1985. I became interested in their ancient beliefs and customs, and on subsequent visits to the Middle East I have attempted to meet with their leaders and to understand their special problems as a minority group in an overwhelmingly Islamic region.

Two of the Coptic participants in our Defenders conference were women, one a psychiatrist and the other a university professor. They gave me a doctrinal booklet entitled *Women*. It summarized the premise that women are equal to men in all religious and secular affairs— *except* when it comes to leadership roles in the Church. This has helped me understand the policies of Roman Catholic and other, more orthodox Christians that prohibit a woman from being ordained as a priest or deacon. I do not agree with this distinction, but I include key excerpts here because so many of my fellow Christians hold this belief and because the text includes some intriguing comments.

Overwhelmingly the treatise disagrees with sexual discrimination derived from the Bible. It explains biblical teachings of sexual equality and also outlines economic history to show the waxing and waning of a woman's role in family life. It begins by stating:

> Man is created twice: The first creation: "God created man in His own image, in the image of God He created him; male and female He created them." (Genesis 1:27) The second creation described by Jesus: "Truly, truly, I say to you, unless one is born of water and the Spirit, he cannot enter the kingdom of God. That which is born of the flesh is flesh, and that which is born of the Spirit is spirit." (John 3:5, 6) The first creation is physical and there is a clear distinction between the male and female sexes, but with no partiality, for both express the image of God. The second creation has no distinction between male and female, for it is a purely spiritual creation. "There is neither male nor female; for you are all one in Christ Jesus." (Galatians 3:28)

The Coptic authors proceed to explain that over time men assumed dominion in the home because they were better suited to hunting, carrying heavy loads, and physically protecting the weaker women and children. When machines were introduced, women found them to be "fearful and dangerous." Men thus used the power of machines to establish their own strength and authority, though in fact the power of the machine was replacing that of man, for the responsibility of running a machine does not depend on physical strength. At this point women woke up and discovered the rights they had lost through their own passivity, revealing the truth of the original statement that God's blessing was granted at the creation to men and women equally and that authority was given to them equally, on condition that they work together in harmony and unity toward a single aim. Equality was proven when women began to be involved in the struggle for a living, learning, and employment and attained the levels of achievement that had for long ages been reserved by men: "The success women attained in every field returned to them all the rights they had surrendered in the false belief that they were created inferior to men."

In the explanation of Paul's letter to the Galatians quoted above, the treatise says, "He deliberately uses the words 'male' and 'female' rather than 'man' and 'woman' to eliminate all aspects of differentiation or discrimination. . . . When a woman is united with Christ she is exactly like a man who is united to Christ, and if a man is united to a woman in Christ, they become in Christ one perfect human being. . . . The Holy Spirit, moreover, does not eliminate the beauty of the first creation, but removes its pitfalls and restores it to its original perfection."

In many places the New Testament describes how Jesus ignored the lowly place of women among Jewish leaders, such as the pious Pharisee who "gave thanks to God every day in his morning prayers that he was not born 'a woman or a leper or an unclean gentile.'" Christ forgave the woman sentenced to death for her adultery, treated as an equal the Samaritan woman who was an outcast among her own despised people by drinking from her cup and sending her into the village as one of the first known evangelists, and appreciated the loyal support of a group of women who "followed him wherever he went and served him in every way they could." Referring to Jesus' followers, the religious pamphlet adds, "The appearance of the women and their going about openly among the crowds, leaving their homes, was a significant event in Israel since it represented an overthrow of the Jewish traditions concerning women and formed part of the official complaint lodged against Christ, which led to his crucifixion: 'We found this man perverting our nation.'" (Luke 23:2)

When the followers of Christ were suffused with the Holy Spirit at the time of Pentecost, the Bible says, "All these with one accord devoted themselves to prayer, together with the women and Mary the mother of Jesus, and with his brothers." (Acts 1:14) The treatise declares:

> The coming of the Holy Spirit upon the women in the same way as He came upon the men, and his filling the women in the same way as He filled the men, is the first permanently effective indication that women had entered into grace and were to be granted equal rights with men in the Kingdom of God. . . . God was aware of how degraded, isolated and abused women had become throughout the ages of the natural law, when man was living by simple skills and was of limited understanding. He Himself took the initiative in order to strike off the fetters that human society had placed on women's hands as on the hands of slaves.

In the Coptic booklet the apostle Paul's declarations that women should keep their heads covered, not cut their hair or wear jewelry, and refrain from speaking out during public worship or assuming a position of leadership are explained as admonitions to address local disturbances by rude and unruly women at services in some particular early church. Paul is also quoted in his letter to the Romans, where he lists heroines of the early Church. It is the same phrase, *fellow-worker*, that Paul uses to describe his associates in the apostolic mission, including Timothy, Titus, and Epaphroditus. In another letter Paul mentions Euodia and Syntyche and adds, "I ask you also, true yokefellow, help these women, for they have labored side by side with me in the Gospel together with

Clement and the rest of my fellow workers whose names are in the book of life." (Philippians 4:2, 3) The Coptic treatise adds, "It is noteworthy that the names of Euodia and Syntyche come before the name of Clement, who became pope of Rome."

This interesting document concludes its analysis of the status of women by rationalizing the policy of the Orthodox Church about excluding women as priests: "So just as the Apostles' wives went with them, having a mission complementary to that of the Apostles in serving the women, just as prophetesses arose in the church alongside the men prophets according to the Gift of the Holy Spirit, though to serve the women, and just as the older women served the church in the same way as older men, and all these with no special ordination rite, so we find alongside the deacons, deaconesses to teach the women also with no special rite of ordination. That is to say, for every service carried out by men there is a service allotted to women." To me, this argument ignores the fact that women prominent in the New Testament ministered to both men and women and leads to the impractical conclusion that there should be separate churches for male and female worshipers, with women apostles, priests, deacons, and bishops leading the worship services attended by women and girls. There are good arguments to be made on both sides of the question of women being equal in serving God, but there can be no justification in extrapolating this to discriminate against and abuse women in our secular society.

I am sure this theological debate will continue about the proper treatment of women, within the Coptic Church and throughout Christendom, and I am equally certain that the words and actions of Jesus Christ will eventually prevail.

We call on all religious leaders throughout the world to take a firm stand and collectively commit to promoting the basic rights of girls and women. This will constitute one of the most important movements in religious history, leading to peace and well-being in our societies. It is a responsibility of any sincere religious leader who seeks to make this world a better place to live. The Carter Center can help bring leaders and people of conscience together for this purpose in a way that will sustain these difficult but necessary efforts to advance equality, justice, dialogue, and peace—across cultures, nations, and continents to assure that our efforts are universal.

SHEIKH MUHAMED CHÉRIF DIOUP,

ISLAMIC RIGHTS SPECIALIST AND

CHILD PROTECTION OFFICER, TOSTAN, SENEGAL

We had several Jewish participants in our Human Rights Defenders Forum, and they described some of the same historical trends and sharp debates among Jewish religious scholars who interpret Holy Scriptures in different ways. The status of the ultra-Orthodox, or Haredim, has changed dramatically since I first visited Israel as governor, primarily because of their high birthrate. They now comprise about 10 percent of the total population and, if current rates continue, are expected to increase to 30 percent in the next three decades. Although some originally refused to become involved in politics, they later formed a number of parties with increasing influence, and in Israel's special form of parliamentary government it has been necessary to include these relatively small groups to give the governing leaders a majority in the Knesset (parliament). This became a matter of sharp debate in the election of January 2013, when the party led by a newcomer to politics, Yair Lapid, won a surprising second place. One of his most popular campaign promises was to eliminate some of the special privileges of the Haredim. To some degree, this issue had been called to public attention by the Haredim's policy of restraining the freedom of women.

The ultra-Orthodox in Israel have always been given tacit permission to control their own neighborhoods, and when they lived in relatively small and clearly defined areas there were few problems. But as their ranks have swelled and different Jewish religious groups have become more integrated within communities, the Haredim's enforcement of strict dress codes, even among passersby on the streets and students entering and leaving schools, has resulted in verbal and physical attacks on women and girls who dress conservatively but in ways that the more strict sects of Haredim consider indecent. Large posters warn women to dress "modestly," and on some bus lines non-Orthodox women are forced to sit in the rear seats or are sometimes forbidden to ride at all. Visual images of women or girls are not permitted, and some ultra-Orthodox men consider it improper to have a nonrelated woman near them or to hear a woman sing or speak in public. This has caused some highly publicized confrontations, especially among the few who are serving in the military. Some women's insistence on worshiping at the Wailing Wall has caused additional personal conflict and resulted in cases now being decided in the judicial system.

These encounters among Israelis of different religious groups have grown increasingly serious, and many are now being resolved through the courts, with some early decisions seeming to be in favor of women's rights. The basic issues are still in doubt and can be resolved only by seminal laws that are being considered by the Knesset concerning the special status of ultra-Orthodox believers and how they are permitted to practice their faith among neighbors who have different beliefs. More women candidates have sought and won seats in the Knesset and now make up 23 percent of its members. There are no women included in the lists of the ultra-Orthodox parties and little indication that wives or daughters in these families are demanding more political or personal rights. It is interesting that 60 percent of these women are in the workforce, while only 45 percent of the men have jobs. There are special government grants to help these devout families support themselves.

As with Christians and Muslims, Jews have come to realize that the basic rights of women are strongly affected by how men choose to interpret and apply the meaning of Holy Scripture. When our mothers, wives, sisters, and daughters are considered both different and inferior in the eyes of the God we worship, this belief tends to permeate society and everyone suffers.

It is difficult for me, as an American Christian, to understand how deprivation of women's rights in Muslim countries can best be confronted and alleviated. At our Human Rights Defenders Forums we listen attentively to participants from different religions and geographical areas, but we refrain from any involvement in their affairs unless requested. One of the most competent and courageous contributors has been Zainah Anwar, who is a defender of human rights for women in Malaysia. She has concentrated on the actual teachings of the Koran and emphasizes that the sacred text of Islam is her most powerful asset. "I am outraged that my religion is distorted and used to justify patriarchy and the discrimination and oppression of women. This totally contradicts what I believe in a just God and a just Islam," she says.

The problem of using a distorted interpretation of Holy Scripture to repress women has been addressed only recently in Western nations, but it began in the 1970s in Malaysia, where women were beginning to receive higher education and become economically independent, and some religious leaders saw this as a threat to their authority. That is when Anwar became active. In 1988 she organized a group called Sisters in Islam (SIS), which petitions the government to reform sexist laws, organizes major conferences, trains women on existing laws and how some contradict their religion, and publicizes their beliefs and activities. They revisit the original teachings of the Koran to prove there is no basis in Islam for viewing women as inferior to men. Anwar explains, "A bunch of us decided that it was really important to find out whether our religion is oppressive toward women, because that's not how we've been brought up to understand Islam."

These women decided not to depend on human rights techniques that were used in the West but to concentrate on the original teachings of the Koran and its message of equality. SIS members point out, "In Islam, everyone is treated equally, and no one comes before the other, and certainly nobody comes from anybody's broken rib. Creation is always spoken of in the Koran in terms of pairs—both are created equal and both are created at the same time, and one is not the derivative of the other." It is not surprising that SIS has earned trust and gratitude in other Islamic countries, as pointed out by Rakhee Goyal, executive director of the Women's Learning Partnership, a nongovernmental organization that works with Muslim women in many regions: "They are at the forefront of study not just in Malaysia but also within Muslim majority societies in looking at how we define the role of women vis-à-vis Islam."

When appropriate, SIS supplements its emphasis on religious law with arguments based on international human rights covenants, national laws, and local social issues. Anwar and her SIS associates are working actively in northwest Africa, Indonesia, the Philippines, and Singapore and have played an important role in the work of The Carter Center. She says, "There is a whole variety of opinions, different interpretations, a multiplicity of laws—this splendid diversity that is part of the Muslim heritage provides us with an incredibly rich source of information, scholarship, and opinion that we can work with to promote our belief in an Islam that upholds the principles of justice and equality, of freedom and dignity."

The work of SIS has aroused opposition in Malaysia, where recent Islamic laws have tended to restrict women's property rights, make polygamy and divorce easier for men, and subvert efforts to thwart domestic violence legislation. This presents Malaysian women with a dilemma, says Anwar. "The choice before us is: Do we accept what these kinds of mullahs are saying, or if we want to be a feminist, do we then reject our religion? For us, rejecting our religion in order to become a feminist is just not a choice. We want to be feminists, and we want to be Muslim as well."

She emphasizes that it is counterproductive for SIS to be too closely associated with Western ideals or organizations:

That [kind of support] doesn't help because those who are not familiar with our work see us as the kind of group that the West wants to develop in Muslim countries. We are not a product of the West; we are a product of our own society and the challenges that we face within our own society. One way for the West to play a productive role is to encourage comprehensive scholarly inquiry into the Islamic canon by developing stronger transnational links between universities. Some of the best work by Muslim scholars is occurring at colleges in the United States and Europe, and these researchers need to be given a platform to speak in places where moderate Islam is under threat. The scholarship that is emerging in the West now is extremely important, and to expose that scholarship, that new thinking, to Muslims in Muslim countries is important.

Upon returning to Ghana after participating in the Carter Center human rights conference, "Mobilizing Faith for Women," we were asked: "Are you on a genuine mission to empower women and make them more productive to support their husbands and families while in marriage? Or are you being paid by your white masters to advance the course of women who develop to become unmanageable, uncontrollable and independent from men?" This is very worrisome because it illustrates the fundamental reasons why we decided to struggle for the rights of the disadvantaged in our communities. The solution is advocacy and training at the top level of Islamic leadership in developing countries. Assisting Imams, Islamic scholars, Muslim chiefs, and opinion leaders as well as youth leaders in this way will advance understand-

ing of the struggle for the empowerment of women and all of
us who believe in human rights for all.

ALHAJI KHUZAIMA, EXECUTIVE SECRETARY,

ISLAMIC PEACE AND SECURITY COUNCIL IN GHANA

I was pleased when Pope John Paul II accepted my invitation to visit
me during his tour of America in 1979. I remembered that when John
Kennedy was campaigning to be the first Catholic president, his critics
had predicted that the pope would be a guest in the White House, and
in my welcoming speech I remarked that this dire prediction had finally come true. During his stay the pope and I had a long and quite relaxed and informal conversation, as he had requested. We talked about
political issues with which I was dealing at the time, a possible visit by
him to Jerusalem and the West Bank, religious developments in China
in which we both were involved, and our mutual hope that growing
competition between Roman Catholics and evangelical Protestants in
Latin America would be without rancor.

When I brought up the subjects of the use of condoms to combat
sexual diseases or the status of women in the Church, I found him surprisingly conservative concerning any possible changes in Church practice. I asked him if the Catholic Church had gotten stronger or weaker
in the previous five years or so, and he replied that it dipped following
Vatican II because of the dramatic changes made in Church liturgy and
the opinion of many believers that the Church had become too liberal,
but he thought it was regaining influence and strength, at least in some
parts of the world, as more traditional values were reemphasized. I was
aware of the plea of some American nuns to the pope of "the possibility
of women . . . being included in all ministries of the church" but didn't
pursue this matter further.

Made up of about 80 percent of Catholic nuns in the United States,
the Leadership Conference of Women Religious (LCWR) was formed
in 1956 with approval from the Vatican "to assist its members [to] carry
out public services of leadership to further the mission of the Gospel
of Jesus Christ in today's world." Its other avowed goals are to foster

dialogue and collaboration within the Church and in the larger community and to strengthen relationships with groups concerned with the needs of society, thereby enhancing the potential for effecting change. This relatively progressive commitment was reinforced by the results of Vatican II (1962–65), which was convened under Pope John XXIII, when some of the more stringent controls of the Vatican were loosened and there was an implication that the Church would accommodate more influence from sisters. In 1979, during the visit of Pope John Paul II to the United States, the president of LCWR made a formal plea for more involvement of women. Since then, most Church leaders have continued to emphasize "bedroom" issues, including abortion, birth control, and homosexuality, and have also affirmed a rigid adherence to the traditional role of women that excludes their admission to the priesthood or other positions of authority. It is estimated that there are now only about a third the number of nuns in America as during the time of Vatican II, but they remain active and have made some specific requests for consideration.

Despite being told by the Vatican to stop talking about their ordination as deacons or priests, some nuns have continued to demand more gender equality in the Catholic Church. In February 2009 the Vatican under Pope Benedict XVI announced that a "doctrinal assessment" of the LCWR would be conducted because of the tenor of their official statements and the content of certain speeches at the organization's annual assemblies. After the assessment was completed, an archbishop from Seattle was appointed to oversee changes in the LCWR to correct what were considered to be positions that differed from Church teachings on sexuality and "certain radical feminist themes incompatible with the Catholic faith."

The sisters pushed back. They have denied any radical feminist tendencies, misbehavior, or deviation from the Church's position on any issue, and explained their reasoning behind previous positions. Some of them expressed a belief that the present pontiff, Pope Francis, was not adequately informed about the history of the dispute between themselves and the Vatican, and in May 2013 the pope made a statement intended to correct what he considered to be a mistake and demanded obedience to the Church and its doctrines, citing this as inseparable from the divinity of Jesus Christ. This dispute within the Church is still unresolved, but some nuns, if not the LCWR officially, seem resolute, especially in their request for women to be included in all ministries of the Church. A group called the Women's Ordination Conference works solely for the ordination of women as priests, deacons, and bishops.

Dr. Phyllis Zagano of Hofstra University sent me the following statement on the subject, which seems to be correct but is perhaps optimistic:

> The Catholic Church requires that individuals with real authority be clerics, that is, ordained persons. The ordinary means of entering the clerical state is by ordination to the diaconate. Despite the Church's objections to ordaining women as priests, discussion about restoring women to the ordained diaconate—an ancient Christian tradition—continues to grow internationally, especially after Pope Francis gave a fairly unqualified "yes" to the concept on his plane ride back from the 2013 World Youth day in Rio de Janeiro. More recently, in August, the pope said, directly, "It is necessary to widen the space for more incisive feminine presence in the church." Catholic deacons are charged with ministry of the Word, the Liturgy, and Charity. They cannot celebrate Eucharist (say Mass) or hear confessions, but can baptize and witness marriages, proclaim the Gospel during Mass, and can hold certain Church offices. More importantly, ordained persons—in this case deacons, who serve *in persona Christi servi* (in the person of Christ, servant)—represent the Risen Christ. For the Catholic Church to ordain a woman and have that woman proclaim the Gospel in St. Peter's would send the strongest possible message to the world that women are made in the image and likeness of God, that women can and do represent Christ.

Nuns are not the only Catholics convinced that women should be permitted to serve as deacons and priests. A public opinion poll by CBS News and the *New York Times* in 2013 reported that 70 percent of U.S. Catholics believe that Pope Francis should authorize women to become priests. There are also a number of long-serving and dedicated priests who have expressed this belief. One of the most noteworthy is Father Roy Bourgeois, who was ordained in 1972 and assigned to work in a slum near La Paz in Bolivia. He was arrested and deported when he criticized the Bolivian dictator, Hugo Banzer, for abuse of poor people, and he then turned his attention to an example of oppression in El Salvador. When Archbishop Oscar Romero was assassinated and four nuns were raped and murdered by Salvadoran military troops who had been trained at Fort Benning, Georgia, Father Bourgeois demonstrated against American involvement in strengthening dictatorships throughout Latin America. He was arrested, convicted, and sentenced to serve eighteen months in prison. The military training program continued and the *Washington Post* reported that techniques of torture were added to the curriculum in 1982. In 1989 U.S.-trained graduates led troops into Jesuit University in San Salvador and killed six priests, plus their servants.

In 1995 Father Bourgeois wrote a letter to Pope John Paul II, urging that priests be permitted to marry and that women be treated as equals. Two years later he participated in a conference in Rome and repeated this proposal during a public radio broadcast. There was no response from the Vatican, but after he took part in the ordination as a priest of Janice Sevre-Duszynska in Lexington, Kentucky, in 2008, he was notified that he had brought "grave scandal" to the Church and would be excommunicated if he did not recant. He replied that he could not betray his conscience, and continued his role as priest and public supporter of equal rights for women. Three years later he received a similar notice from his immediate superior, with a fifteen-day deadline for compliance. He responded that he had been a Catholic priest for thirty-nine years and added, "In my ministry over the years I have met many devout women in our Church who believe God is calling them to be priests. Why wouldn't they be called? God created men and women of equal dignity and, as we all know, the call to be a priest comes from God." He joined an international delegation that went to the Vatican to deliver a petition from fifteen thousand supporters of women's ordination as priests, and in November 2012 he received a final official notice that he was "dispensed of his sacred bonds" as a priest. Father Bourgeois stated that he regretted the decision but was filled with hope that women will one day be treated as equal to men.

The Vatican's position can best be described by an edict issued in May 2010, "Normae de gravioribus delictis," that the attempted sacred ordination of a woman is one of the gravest substantive canonical crimes in the Church, on a par with sexually abusing a child. (Very few priests have been excommunicated who were found guilty of child abuse.) Although there is no current sign, even from newly chosen Pope Francis, that rigid Church doctrine is likely to change, there are some practical trends that may force reconsideration in the future. One is the obvious and almost universal practice of Catholic families of ignoring the mandate against the use of contraceptives to limit family size; another is the knowledge that the prohibition against the use of condoms contributes to the spread of AIDS. Bishops and priests look the other way when contraception is practiced in Africa and other regions and do not confront the issue when their own parishes are involved. A troubling trend within the Church organization is the growing shortage of celibate men who come forward to be priests and the possible effect this sexual restraint has had on the worldwide scandal of priests found guilty of child abuse. There are now more than fifty thousand parishes in the world that do not have an assigned priest, and the need for more parish leaders is even greater in the United States, where the number of priests has steadily dropped, from 58,909 in 1975 to fewer than 39,600 in 2013.

It is known that the first pope, Saint Peter, was married, because Jesus healed his mother-in-law. Because of these kinds of biblical premises and other pressures to emulate the ministry of Christ among parishioners, there may come a time when Catholic priests are permitted to marry and qualified women are called to serve God on an equal basis. Until that time, the enormous influence of the Church could be used forcefully to condemn sexual assaults, genital cutting, child marriage, inadequate pay for women, honor killings, and deprivation of equal rights for women in economic and political affairs. I have written a letter to Pope Francis outlining these opportunities to improve the status of women without addressing the sensitive issue of women as priests. In the Vatican's response, His Holiness thanked me for my concern and reiterated his insistence on "the need to create still broader opportunities for a more incisive female presence in the Church." He also believes that "demands that the legitimate rights of women be respected, based on the firm conviction that men and women are equal in dignity, present the Church with profound and challenging questions which cannot be evaded."

I am pleased that many other Christian denominations are modifying outmoded traditions and responding to pressure from individual worshipers by treating women as equal to men in all aspects of religious life. As is the custom in some Baptist churches, members of our congregation meet in conference to make all significant decisions, including the democratic election of pastors, deacons, and committee members. As I mentioned earlier, we have a male and a female pastor, and half of our deacons are women (including my wife). Our church is affiliated with the Cooperative Baptist Fellowship, and the recently elected leader of this denomination is also a woman. It has long been customary to have women as pastors among African American churches, and in November 2013 the governing body of the Anglican Church voted to move forward a proposal to allow the appointment of women bishops; a final vote will likely take place in 2014. This is part of a general and inexorable trend among Methodists, Presbyterians, Episcopalians, Lutherans, and other major Protestant denominations in all nations to adopt this same enlightened policy. There have been extended and sometimes heated debates in their annual conferences, but ultimately the collective will has prevailed. It seems that those who are resisting change are losing both numbers and influence among their members in crucial societal matters.

10 | THE GENOCIDE OF GIRLS

During our 1981 visit to rural China, we found local officials very proud of their strictly enforced family planning program. The nation's population then was just exceeding a billion, and the common slogan throughout China was "One is best, two at most." We were already familiar with attempts to control the population in another large country, when my mother served as a Peace Corps volunteer in India. Prime Minister Indira Gandhi requested that as a registered nurse she teach sex education to poor families and assist the local doctor in performing mandatory vasectomies on fathers after their first child. Mama objected but had to comply.

In China we saw a number of billboards and posters depicting two happy parents walking through a public park or other nice place and proudly holding the hands of their only child. In every case the child was a boy. At the time, we presumed that this was just the choice of the photographer, but over the years I have come to realize that parents' special pride in a male child would have serious consequences.

Historically, on a global basis, slightly more males than females have been born, a natural disparity that anthropologists and demographers cannot explain. In a few nations, however, there has been a significant deviation from this ratio, indicating the result of a preference for boys. World Health Organization data show that in India the ratio of girls to boys is 100 to 112. When sex ratio studies began in China in 1960, they found 100 females to 106 males, near the upper border of the normal range. In 1990 the discrepancy had increased to 100 females to 112 males, and by 2010 the ratio was 100 to 118. The *PBS News Hour* reports that in some areas of India there are only 650 girl babies living for every 1,000 boys, a ratio of 100 to 154! Infanticide, either at the time of birth or later, seems to be the cause. With the availability of sonogram examinations, a new option was presented to parents, who can ascertain the sex of a developing fetus as early as twelve weeks after conception. Inexpensive sonograms can now be hooked up to laptop computers and are widely available even in remote rural areas. In some places the abortion of female fetuses is relatively easy and legal and has even been encouraged.

When these percentages are multiplied by the total number of children born in some of the world's largest nations, the number of girls that have been eliminated by abortion, neglect, or murder is horrendous. The Indian Nobel Laureate Amartya Sen estimated in 1990 that there were 50 million females "missing" in China, and more than 105 million worldwide. Almost all of the decisions to terminate the existence of these girls were made privately, within families, and not ordained by governments. Shadowline Films produced a documentary entitled *It's a Girl* that had its Hong Kong premiere in November 2013. One episode presents a mother in India who states calmly that she has strangled eight of her newborn daughters. This selective murder of girls is called *female gendercide* or *femicide*.

In India sexual discrimination also occurs among children who survive birth. A UN Children's Fund report issued in October 2013 reveals that India accounts for 20 percent of child mortality worldwide. Although there has been some improvement in recent years, India's under-five child mortality rate in 2012 was 56 deaths per 1,000. By comparison, the rate in equally poor Bangladesh was 41; in Brazil, 14; and in the United States, 7. A special tragedy is that 131 little girls died in India compared to each 100 boys of the same age.

Efforts in India, China, and South Korea to outlaw gendercide or the use of sonograms for the same purpose have been predictably unsuccessful. Mara Hvistendahl is a contributing editor to *Science* magazine, and in 2012 she wrote *Unnatural Selection: Choosing Boys over Girls, and the Consequences of a World Full of Men*. In this carefully researched book, she estimates that there are now at least 160 million missing females. This is equivalent to an entire generation of girls being wiped from the face of the earth. To put this into perspective, it is estimated that 500,000 Tutsis were killed in the Rwanda genocide of 1994, and that 6 million Jews were victims of the Nazi Holocaust.

Most of these lethal decisions are still concentrated in the Asian countries mentioned above, but the option of femicide is also exercised in smaller nations and in the more advanced Western world. It appears that more than twice as many girls have been killed by their parents during my lifetime as the total number of combatants and civilians lost in World War II.

One unanticipated result has been a disturbing shortage of brides and a demand for prostitutes to assuage the desires of men without partners. News reports from South Korea indicate that imported brides from less affluent Asian nations are selling for a high price. The latest data show that 12 percent of all marriages of South Korean men are with foreign women from Vietnam, Cambodia, the Philippines, and Japan. There is a thriving market, with the price of a bride ranging from US$88 to US$660. The girls' parents receive from US$11 to US$22. The organization Human Rights in China reports that it is usually cheaper to buy a bride from traffickers for about US$320 to US$640 than to pay the normal bride price, which is often two to five times higher. Chinese police report that an average of 17,500 women who were sold into marriage or slavery against their will are rescued each year. Between 1991 and 1996, 143,000 human traffickers were arrested and prosecuted.

This pervasive elimination of girls, both before and after birth, is obvious and well known, but it continues. Preventive laws have been ineffective, and the only apparent solution is to convince parents that a daughter can, in all respects, be an asset to the family. This can be accomplished only by ensuring that girls are educated and given equal opportunities to develop their talents, to earn an income, and to serve their family and community.

11 | RAPE

According to the U.S. Justice Department, there were 191,610 cases of rape or sexual assault in the United States in 2006, and 91 percent of the victims were female. That's more than 475 women assaulted every day. The estimate is that only 16 percent of these cases are reported to the police; the rate drops to fewer than 5 percent on college campuses. Girls and women of all ages and all backgrounds suffer from the same or worse sexual violence throughout the world, and some traditional practices constitute, extol, and perpetuate sexual violence against women and girls.

Radha Kumar is an author and expert on ethnic conflicts and has been a director at the Nelson Mandela Centre for Peace and Conflict Resolution in New Delhi. She describes rape in India as one of the nation's most common crimes against women, and the UN's High Commissioner for Human Rights asserts that it is a "national problem." India's National Crime Records Bureau reports that rape cases have doubled between 1990 and 2008. There were 24,206 cases registered in India in 2011 (one every twenty-two minutes), and many attacks go unreported. The gang rape in Delhi of a twenty-three-year-old student on a bus in December 2012 is one of the most horrible examples: she was raped by several men, who then used an iron rod to penetrate her genitals so deeply that her intestines had to be surgically removed. She died thirteen days later.

There was a tremendous public outcry in India and abroad, and in September 2013 the rapists were sentenced to be hanged. Many have supported the sentence, but human rights activists are raising the alarm that executing these men might actually harm the cause of women's rights. Divya Iyer, a senior researcher at Amnesty International, makes a compelling case: "The death penalty does not offer a transformative idea in a social context where violence against women often involves notions of honor. It does not change patriarchal attitude and feudal mindset that trivialize and condone violence against women—be it from the man on the bus or a senior politician. . . . The debate around the death penalty deflects attention from the harder procedural and institutional reform that the government must bring about to tackle violence against women more effectively." This gets to the heart of the matter. Effective law enforcement is crucial, but financial and human resources are not expended on those government functions that actually will prevent sexual violence.

It seems remarkable that such violence is occurring in a Hindu society in which there are many female deities and in which the Sanskrit saying "Mata, Pita, Guru, Deva" (Mother, Father, Teacher, God) emphasizes how prominent are mothers in the life of a Hindu family. In August 2013 the *New York Times* ran an intriguing article by Vinita Bharadwaj, an Indian journalist now based in Dubai who described her life in India as being subject to "stares, glares, whistles, hoots, shout-outs, songs, 'accidental' brushing-past, intentional grabbing, groping and pinching" by men. In addition to enforcement of the existing laws by police and the courts, she writes, "what India desperately needs is a women's revolution, led by men—fathers, sons, grandfathers, brothers, uncles, nephews, boyfriends, husbands, and lovers who are comfortable with the rise of their women. It's a change that must begin in our homes."

In 1994 the world witnessed the terrible slaughter by extremist Hutus in Rwanda of an estimated 500,000 ethnic Tutsis and thousands of Hutus who opposed the killing campaign. Retribution came quickly as Tutsi-led rebel forces routed the Hutu government forces causing an evacuation of the country by Hutus fearing further retribution. A million Hutus fled across the border into eastern Zaire, many to a massive refugee camp in the city of Goma. Large numbers also fled east to Tanzania. All the nations of the Great Lakes region (Uganda, Tanzania, Kenya, Zaire, Rwanda, and Burundi) suffered greatly from the upheaval and violence. Former Hutu soldiers in the refugee camps rearmed and began raiding across the Zaire-Rwanda border.

When United Nations efforts to bring about a regional peace conference collapsed in 1995, the leaders of the Great Lakes region reached out to me and The Carter Center. We explored what needed to be done. Rosalynn and I visited the enormous refugee camp in Goma, where large numbers of people moved in and out, and the small staff made it clear that very little order could be maintained. Rape and abuse of women were rampant. The Carter Center launched a major effort to bring peace. We brought together all the presidents of the region in Cairo in November 1995 and in Tunis in March 1996. Agreements were reached that should have moved the region forward. However, international support was not forthcoming and the agreements were not implemented.

The ramifications included a terrible civil war in Zaire. The victor, Laurent-Désiré Kabila, named himself president and changed the name of the country back to the Democratic Republic of the Congo (DRC). Kabila was assassinated in 2001 and was succeeded by his son Joseph.

The Carter Center has continued its interest in the DRC, and we have monitored two nationwide elections since then. The 2006 election was well run and relatively free and fair, but the election five years later was marred by misconduct and resulted in a crisis of legitimacy for the reelected President Kabila. Throughout this time the Rwandan government has supported militia forces in eastern Congo in order to promote its interests there, including the transfer of Congo's bountiful precious minerals to overseas markets.

The terrible aftermath of these military and political events has been one of the worst epidemics of rape in history, as Tutsi, Hutu, and Congolese militiamen surge back and forth in control of disputed territory and systematically and brazenly abuse women in the areas they control. In addition to sexual gratification, the soldiers use bottles, sticks, and even bayonets to torture the women and to declare their masculine supremacy. They treat this practice as a prerogative of warfare. In November 2012 Congolese troops trained by the U.S. government perpetrated a mass rape of 135 women and girls in the eastern town of Minova, which received little response from the international community. The Congo has become known as the "world capital of rape." Despite this terrible sexual carnage, neither the secretary-general nor the UN Security Council has chosen to make these crimes a top priority.

There is a remarkable incidence of rape in the region of southern Africa, as recorded by the South African Medical Research Council in 2009 and by the *Lancet Global Health* journal in 2013. Interviews of thousands of men revealed that more than 20 percent in Tanzania, 26 percent in South Africa, and 34 percent in eastern Congo had "forced a woman not [their] wife or girlfriend to have sex." In most other developing nations, only 2 to 4 percent of men gave this response, and the level was lower in the industrialized world. The basic causes for this sexual abuse against women and girls were determined to be the combination of a strongly patriarchal society, tribal divisions, minimal law enforcement, and extreme poverty. Official condemnation by the UN Security Council and enforcement of the International Violence Against Women Act (IVAWA) and other laws are the only potential remedies for this plague of violence. As will be seen, there is encouraging progress in this area being made by a British diplomat and a Holly-wood actress.

The blame for sexual abuse is often placed on the victim. We have 776 citizens living in Plains, and there are usually between seventy-five and a hundred Hispanics; almost all have legal work permits and jobs in local companies, but only a few are American citizens. Our small church has a regular ministry among the most deprived families of all races, using funds from the sale of audio and video tapes of my Bible lessons. Rosalynn participates in the monthly visits to about thirty homes at a time. The Hispanic workers are especially dedicated to their jobs and are extremely careful not to violate any laws because they do not wish to be deported. Under Georgia's oppressive legislation, they are not permitted to obtain a driver's license and therefore have to walk or ride a bicycle to their job or to do their shopping. They send as much of their income as possible back to their families in Latin America, and occasionally some will make a bus trip to visit their home country.

Recently one of our church friends returned to Mexico, leaving his wife and children in Plains. A man broke into their home, threatened the children, and raped their mother. She called our pastor, who reported the crime to the local police and also to her husband. The rapist evaded the authorities, and the husband blamed his wife for the rape and refused to return. The wife and children feared for their safety and moved to another town about thirty miles away to live with an aunt. Blaming the victim, even among my neighbors, is all too common.

Myanmar (formerly Burma) suffered under a despotic military dictatorship for more than fifty years, but the election of 2011 resulted in legitimately chosen leaders, almost all former high military officers who initiated a remarkable transformation toward freedom and democracy. As the country moves toward its next election in 2015,

The Carter Center will maintain a permanent presence to observe the electoral process and to assist as requested in overcoming the many challenges still facing the different ethnic and religious groups that are learning to live together in a more liberated society. One of the most formidable problems is the conflict that has erupted as the overwhelming Buddhist majority dominates the minority Muslims in Rakhine State near Bangladesh and Christians who are concentrated mostly in Kachin State on the border with China.

A related challenge is to formulate cease-fire agreements between the central government and more than a dozen regional ethnic groups and then to write a permanent constitution that will guarantee political, economic, and social equity among them.

I have visited Myanmar twice while writing this book and have learned from multiple sources how women and girls are bearing the brunt of the existing conflict and discrimination. I met with leaders of religious groups who are Roman Catholic, Protestant, Muslim, Hindu, and Buddhist and found them compatible with each other. When I asked them about the status of women, almost all responded that within their religious group "women are treated as equals—but considered to be either separate or different." This reminded me of my childhood days, when black people were legally considered "separate but equal." They were kept largely separate and certainly not treated as equals.

Still existing in Myanmar are camps for internally displaced persons who have been forced from their homes by strife or prejudice. I was given the results of a scholarly study conducted in Kachin State of the special problems of women and girls among this group. It is particularly interesting because it is the only study I have found that describes the situation that likely prevails in most camps for displaced persons and refugees in the world. With very few separate facilities for toilets, sleeping, or bathing, all sexual encounters are fraught with violence and danger, and the consumption of alcohol and drugs aggravates the situation. There are no doors to separate living areas, but only flaps of canvas and cloth. Children of all ages are in danger when left alone by their parents, and spousal abuse is common when wives object to a lack of privacy during sex or are fearful of pregnancy because no birth control is available. Women claim that it is fruitless to report sexual abuse because the administrators are usually men and frequently among the worst culprits, and their response to the women is most often laughter or a wave of dismissal. Any remaining restraints are ignored when a cease-fire is broken and armed troops of another tribe or religion invade the area. These abused and fearful women and girls can only pray for a time of peace and law enforcement.

The military is still dominant in Myanmar, with their half-century accumulation of wealth, property, and influence, and also with the right of the top commanding officer to appoint (and peremptorily remove) 25 percent of the members of the Parliament. When I met with him on two visits he extolled the performance of his troops in maintaining order and assisting (but not interfering with) the local police. He said that the only role for women in the military is to serve in the medical corps and that he had never appointed any women to parliamentary seats, but he promised to consider this option in the future. (In January 2014, I was informed that two female officers have been chosen as legislators.)

In areas of conflict between armed combatants or where displaced persons have no homes and are crowded into camps, the prevailing atmosphere of violence is combined with the loss of normal family privacy and mutual protection. Women, children, and other defenseless people become especially vulnerable to abuse. All too often, this tragic situation is condoned by local officials and ignored by the international community.

12 | SLAVERY AND PROSTITUTION

The world experienced a gigantic political, economic, and military struggle during the nineteenth century to end the blight of trafficking in human beings, primarily from Africa to the New World in ships owned by Europeans. During the three and a half centuries of the transatlantic slave trade, it is estimated that 12.5 million slaves were taken from Africa to the Americas. This was a terrible and unforgivable example of abuse of people.

My great-great-grandfather, Wiley Carter, owned several dozen slaves when he died during the last year of the War Between the States. Family records show that when they were freed soon thereafter, his estate lost two-thirds of its monetary value. As I write, we are commemorating the 150th anniversary of the decisive Battle of Gettysburg, where my great-grandfather and his two brothers fought under General Robert E. Lee. The Civil War was the most deadly single event in our nation's history, and there was, at least eventually, a sigh of relief from both sides that the time of slavery was over.

Although there is no longer any legal slavery in the world, the Global Slavery Index report released in October 2013 estimates that 29.8 million people remain enslaved today. Using a broader definition of slavery, this includes those living in bondage as forced laborers, those in marriages against their will, and prostitutes engaged involuntarily in the sexual trade. The UN International Labor Organization reports that there are now approximately 20.9 million people engaged in forced labor. *Foreign Affairs* magazine observes, "Slavery and the global slave trade continue to thrive to this day; in fact, it is likely that more people are being trafficked across borders against their will now than at any point in the past."

Modern slavery generates approximately $32 billion in profits each year, about half of which goes to rich industrialized nations such as our own. The Global Slavery Index listed the United States as currently having almost sixty thousand people in bondage, while Mauritania ranks highest in the percentage of its citizens who are slaves (about 4 percent). When I first visited its capital, Nouakchott, in 1994 and raised the subject, the president and other top officials claimed that they had passed laws to prohibit the crime but admitted that the practice was so ingrained in the culture of some regions that it was impossible to control. More than 1.1 percent of India's citizens are living in bondage, a total of 13,956,010, by far the highest of any nation, with China second at 2,949,243.

Many books have been written about the modern slave trade. The author of one of the most definitive and thoroughly researched is Siddharth Kara, who was born in Tennessee but spent much of his youth in India. He is a former investment banker, business executive, lawyer, and director of Free the Slaves, an organization devoted to exposing and abolishing slavery. He has spent several years of his life traveling to the nations most deeply involved in the procurement, movement, and exploitation of slaves and has conducted thousands of interviews with people living in slavery. Kara has used his business training to estimate the illicit profits derived from these criminal activities within individual regions and countries. Using the same definition as the Slavery Index, he agrees that there are about 30 million people in the world who are living unwillingly under the domination of their masters.

Kara estimates that those who own and operate brothels can acquire a slave prostitute for less than $1,000 in Asia and from $2,000 to $8,000 in Western Europe and North America, with a worldwide average price of $1,900. The annual net profit to the slave's owner is about $29,000. Even in comparison with crime cartels engaged in the drug trade this is an attractive business; whereas cocaine or opium can be consumed only once, the sexual services of a woman can be sold thousands of times each year. Police and other local officials who condone or even participate in prostitution are at much less risk than those assigned to deal with the trade in illicit drugs, and by claiming that the prostitutes are selling their favors freely they can rationalize their complicity in the women's brutal duress. Kara concludes that the best way to combat the sex trade in young women and girls who have been seduced or abducted into forced prostitution is to concentrate on the male customers, who provide the enormous financial profits that keep the slave masters and brothel owners in business.

The U.S. State Department estimates that about 800,000 people are traded across international borders each year, and 80 percent of these victims are women and girls. More than three-fourths of them are sold into the sex trade. During our recent Human Rights Defenders Forum at The Carter Center, it was reported that between two hundred and three hundred children are sold in Atlanta alone each month! Our city is considered to be one of the preeminent human trafficking centers in the United States, perhaps because we have the busiest airport in the world and because, until recently, the penalty for someone convicted of selling another human being was only a $50 fine. A much heavier penalty of up to twenty years' imprisonment can be imposed by the federal government, but only if there is proof that the trafficking took place across state lines.

An analysis by Atlanta social workers found that 42 percent of the sexual exchanges they investigated were in brothels and hotel rooms in the most affluent areas of the city, while only 9 percent were in the poorer neighborhoods in the vicinity of the airport. Like Kara, they too conclude that the primary culprits are the men who buy sexual favors and the male pimps and brothel owners who control the women and garner most of the financial gains. Lax law enforcement, from top political officials to police on the street, is always a crucial element in the sex trade.

Modern social media have resulted in an interesting and tragic development in the field of prostitution in America: housewives and others who sell themselves for sexual purposes through the Internet. Although there are some apparent advantages to the women in eliminating the control of pimps and brothel owners and retaining their entire fee, there can be tragic consequences to operating in an environment that is not familiar to them and without having anyone to provide a modicum of protection. Since their activities are illegal and embarrassing if revealed, they are also unlikely to report brutality or sexual abuse to law enforcement officials.

In July 2013 the *New York Times* ran a feature story entitled "The New Prostitutes" that described the experiences of ten of these women, all of whom had advertised their services on Craigslist, Backpage, TheEroticReview, or one of the hundreds of other available websites. The women met their temporary partners in their own home or in a rented apartment or hotel room. Their rates ranged from $250 to $400 per hour, and they often made as much as $2,000 on a busy night. The bodies of all ten women were found buried in sand dunes or alongside highways on Long Island. Economist Scott Cunningham, at Baylor University, surveyed the sex market in New York City in 2009 and found that an average of 1,690 sex-worker ads were posted online every day.

It is known that teenage girls are sold by pimps and placed in brothels in all large American cities, almost invariably with the local police being complicit or waiting for "more important" things to command their attention. There was no comprehensive law to prosecute domestic or international traffickers in the United States prior to October 2000, when the Trafficking Victims Protection Act (TVPA) was enacted. President George W. Bush announced that the TVPA was designed to (1) prevent human trafficking at home and overseas, (2) protect victims and support them in rebuilding their lives in the United States, and (3) prosecute the traffickers. The law also allows victims of international trafficking to become temporary U.S. residents and avoid immediate deportation. It was strengthened three years later, when $200 million was authorized to combat human trafficking.

It is hard to know how many women and girls are trafficked in India, but the U.S. State Department, the United Nations, and India's Human Rights Commission have identified that country as a major hub in the international sex trade. Poverty is a major factor. Many desperate parents are enticed by promises of training and employment of their daughters, and sell them to traffickers who promise that a portion of the girls' earnings will be returned to them. Rapid urbanization and the migration of large numbers of men into India's growing cities create a market for commercial sex, as does the gender imbalance resulting from sex-selective abortion practices that has created a generation of young men who have little hope of finding a female partner. The relative affluence in some communities is also a factor, luring foreign women into the sex trade. The caste system compounds the problem; many victims of sex trafficking come disproportionately from disadvantaged segments of India's society.

The trafficking of girls from Nepal into India has been the focus of much international attention. UNICEF reported that as many as seven thousand women and girls are trafficked out of Nepal to India every year, and around 200,000 are now working in Indian brothels. They are induced to leave their home communities by promises of lucrative jobs in Kathmandu or across the border in India, marriages to attractive husbands, free education, training to be beauty technicians, teachers, or nurses or to sell popular consumer products. Some girls have been forcefully abducted from the streets. Once in the hands of their traffickers, they are transported to their destination, raped, beaten, or drugged into submission, and then delivered to a brothel to service numerous men each day or to an "owner" who can use them as slaves. Escape is discouraged by warnings of worse physical punishment, incarceration under vigilant supervision, or threats to the girls' families back home.

Top Nepalese law enforcement officials inform me that they know of the many thousands of Nepalese women enslaved in sexual or other servitude every year, but that it is quite easy for the traffickers to obtain false high-quality passports and visas to transport them to rich communities in a foreign country. There are orders from some Arab nations for women who will serve as second or later brides, mostly for the work they will be forced to do within their husband's household. The books I have read about the lucrative global system of slavery always cite Nepal as one of the worst examples. Neither the former monarchy nor the new democracy (still struggling to form a government and draft a constitution) provides protection for poor and vulnerable families, in which parents often bemoan the birth of a daughter and celebrate with the community when the newborn baby is a boy. Every effort is made to educate boys, but fewer than 5 percent of women are literate in some of the poorer communities.

We have visited Nepal several times, to climb in the Himalayas and more recently to help monitor their elections and help them form a government. While there to prepare for the election held in November 2013, Rosalynn and I had an opportunity to meet with a group of young women who had escaped sexual slavery. The organization that was helping with the rescue and providing protection was known as Stop Girl Trafficking (SGT) and was financed largely by a longtime friend of ours, Richard Blum. He and Sir Edmund Hillary, who was the first to climb Mount Everest, are the founders of the American Himalayan Foundation, which has many other benevolent projects in the region. Richard explained to us on the way to Kathmandu that SGT had been working closely with the Rural Health and Education Service Trust (RHEST) for fifteen years. The primary tool that RHEST has found to be effective in sustaining the freedom of the rescued women is to provide them with an education. This restores their self-respect and assures that literacy and marketable skills can sustain them and their families in the future.

The young women who met with us were relaxed and unrestrained as they recounted their experiences and their plans for productive lives in the future. There were outbursts of laughter as they described circumstances or events in their past, which helped to prevent any embarrassment as they discussed some of the intimate details. None had been enrolled in school at the time they were taken into captivity, and they all agreed that their current classrooms were the best places to prepare for the future. Some had not been reconciled with their family after their parents learned of their forced sexual activities, but they were either resigned to the familial estrangement or expressed the hope that their future would improve the relationship. Many of them had been helped to escape from bondage by friends who were familiar with SGT, and they told us that they looked for opportunities to help those who were still enslaved.

The SGT and RHEST leaders expected to have ten thousand women and girls in their program during the year 2013. This will include a large number who had been indentured servants, "rented" by wealthier families from among those people in Nepal who are *dalits* (untouchables). The rich family pays an agent about $50, of which the girl's family gets about $14. Each year a new transaction is concluded. Some are treated well; others are beaten, denied any educational opportunities, and often attacked sexually by the men or boys in the house.

After we thanked the women for their testimonies and had a round of photographs, we heard from administrators of SGT about their efforts to address the root causes of slavery by working for more effective legislation, improving protection for girls in the poorest families, creating public education programs about this cancer in their midst, and offering educational opportunities to the younger girls in the most vulnerable families. There was special concern about the common practice of forced child marriage in Nepal. The interim constitution of 2006 set the legal marriage age of women at twenty, but the penalty for violation is only annulment of the marriage and a fine of $8. The consequence for the child bride is that she is disgraced and unfit for a more appropriate husband. The willing, usually poverty-stricken parents of the girls accede to opportunities to receive a small payment or to reduce the number of mouths they have to feed. A young bride is often not expected to serve as a wife and mother but as just another servant in her new home. When I asked some we met if they would rather be sold into slavery or sold as a child bride, all said that a forced marriage would be the worse of the two terrible choices.

It is important to note that forced prostitution is most prevalent in societies where "nice" girls are strictly protected until marriage. Young men and others turn to prostitutes for sexual gratification and are often able and willing to pay more for younger girls. There is a large bonus for the rare virgin.

Violence against women remains one of the greatest ills of our time. It is shameful that for many women and girls walking in the streets, relaxing in parks, going to work, or even staying at home can become a brutal experience. When women and girls feel unsafe, half of humanity is unsafe. Violence against women and girls is perpetuated by centuries of male dominance and gender-based discrimination. But the roles that have traditionally been assigned to men and women in society are a human construct—there is nothing divine about them. Religious leaders have a responsibility to address these historic injustices. Respect for human dignity should not be dependent on whether one is a male or a female.

MONA RISHMAWI, OFFICE OF THE UNITED NATIONS HIGH COMMISSIONER FOR HUMAN RIGHTS

To address the worldwide problem of millions of people being enslaved, the U.S. State Department is required to file a Trafficking in Persons Report annually to indicate how other nations are combating slavery and to encourage them to be more aggressive in their efforts. The latest report, in 2013, included 188 countries and measured them in three categories, or tiers, according to how well they met eleven benchmarks. Tier 1 includes thirty countries that have met the minimum standards to combat slavery but acknowledge that they can make more progress; tier 2 comprises ninety-two countries that have made some tangible effort but do not meet the minimum standards; and there are twenty-one countries in tier 3 that have taken no affirmative steps to fight human trafficking. These are the eleven criteria:

1. Prohibit trafficking and punish acts of trafficking.
2. Prescribe punishment commensurate with that for other serious crimes.
3. Make serious and sustained efforts to eliminate trafficking.
4. Vigorously investigate and prosecute acts of trafficking.
5. Protect victims of trafficking; encourage victims' assistance in investigation and prosecution.
6. Provide victims with legal alternatives to their removal to punitive countries and ensure that trafficked victims are not inappropriately penalized.
7. Adopt measures, such as public education, to prevent trafficking.
8. Cooperate with other governments in investigating and prosecuting trafficking.
9. Extradite persons charged with trafficking as with other serious crimes.

10. Monitor immigration and emigration patterns for evidence of trafficking, and assure that law enforcement agencies respond to such evidence.

11. Investigate and prosecute public officials who participate, facilitate, or condone trafficking.

U.S. government officials acknowledge that, although our country meets the minimum tier 1 standards, there are many challenges still to be met. In addition to the mostly female sexual slaves that are sold freely in America, there are those in our country who are held as prisoners and forced to work under duress because they have immigrated illegally. Often they owe a large sum of money to the person who transported them that is beyond their means to repay. There is continuing partisan debate in Congress about whether stronger legal protection should apply to Native Americans, undocumented immigrants, and transsexuals forced into prostitution or include counseling or contraceptives to victims of sexual abuse. Some conservative women's organizations and the U.S. Conference of Catholic Bishops oppose the legislation on these grounds.

On a few occasions abused people have taken legal action to protect themselves. For almost twenty years The Carter Center has been attempting to assist the tomato harvesters in Immokalee, Florida, to achieve justice in their working conditions, and we have observed with pride the additional efforts of the Coalition of Immokalee Workers (CIW) to expose wealthy landowners who were holding their farmworkers in involuntary servitude. The CIW helped fight this crime by uncovering and assisting in the federal prosecution of slavery rings preying on hundreds of laborers. In such situations, captive workers were held against their will by their employers for many years through threats and beatings, shootings, and pistol-whippings. In 2010 the CIW followed up these exposés and convictions by developing a mobile Slavery Museum that they brought to Atlanta for us to see and then took it on a tour of the southeastern United States to demonstrate what was happening to poor and defenseless workers.

There needs to be much more vigorous investigation and prosecution of those who are engaged in modern-day slavery. Although seldom utilized, a stringent law exists, as stated in Title 18 of the U.S. Code, Sec. 1589 ("Forced Labor"):

> Whoever knowingly provides or obtains the labor or services of a person
>
> (1) by threats of serious harm to, or physical restraint against, that person or another person;
>
> (2) by means of any scheme, plan, or pattern intended to cause the person to believe that, if the person did not perform such labor or services, that person or another person would suffer serious harm or physical restraint; or
>
> (3) by means of the abuse or threatened abuse of law or the legal process,
>
> shall be fined under this title or imprisoned not more than 20 years, or both. If death results from the violation of this section, or if the violation includes kidnapping or an attempt to kidnap, aggravated sexual abuse or the attempt to commit aggravated sexual abuse, or an attempt to kill, the defendant shall be fined under this title or imprisoned for any term of years or life, or both.

This sounds good, but the law is essentially ignored. Although the U.S. Department of State has estimated that there are at least sixty thousand people being held against their will in the United States, only 138 traffickers were convicted in this country in 2012.

There is something powerful the U.S. government could do, right now, to stop gender-based violence globally. The International Violence Against Women Act (IVAWA), which has awaited action in the U.S. Congress for six years, lies dormant because not enough voices have yet risen to demand its passage. IVAWA would make America a leader in ending violence against women and girls. It would be a new beacon of light for millions of women and children who cower under the hand of an abuser, who dare not attend school because they will be shot, and who remain in a corner of darkness because there is no one to receive them in the light. Let us help receive them. Let us pass IVAWA now.

RITU SHARMA, COFOUNDER AND PRESIDENT,

WOMEN THRIVE WORLDWIDE

It is crucial for political leaders and all of us to understand the inter-relationship among politics, the sex trade, and the general welfare. This can best be demonstrated in Africa, where the AIDS virus originated and where preventative and curative medicines have been introduced in tardy and inadequate ways. Containing only 15 percent of the world's population, 70 percent of those who are HIV-infected and die with AIDS are Africans. Much of the infection, especially in South Africa, has been spread by truck drivers, miners, and other men who work away from home, patronize brothels, and then transmit the disease to their wives and families. I learned about this tragedy on a visit to the continent in 2002.

Bill Gates Sr. was in charge of the enormous foundation established by his son, and he was planning his first visit to Africa in 2002 to meet some of the top leaders and get acquainted with the region and issues in which they planned to invest. He asked Rosalynn and me to accompany him and his wife, Mimi, on a trip around the periphery of the continent so he could learn as much as possible about the devastating AIDS epidemic. At the time, there were two key features of an effective anti-AIDS program: antiretroviral medicines for those who were known to be infected and a public awareness campaign that emphasized the gravity of the epidemic.

We met Bill and Mimi in Johannesburg, South Africa, where about

25 percent of the citizens were suffering from HIV/AIDS, greatly exacerbated by the claim of President Thabo Mbeki that the value of antiretroviral treatments was unproven and they were likely to be toxic and were being foisted on innocent black people by white leaders from Western nations. He had condemned the use of any of these drugs, including the well-proven nevirapine, which can protect babies of HIV mothers from the infection. Our expert on the trip was Dr. Helene Gayle, who had recently left the Centers for Disease Control to head the Gates Foundation's global crusade against HIV/AIDS. She emphasized that nevirapine given to prospective mothers would reduce by half the sixty thousand annual infant AIDS deaths.

We were informed that there would be a meeting in Soweto to publicize the issue, and I decided to invite former president Nelson Mandela to join us. Bill told me that Mandela had expressed doubts about "Western" drugs at a meeting with the Gates Foundation officials in Seattle, Washington, when he was president of South Africa, so I was pleasantly surprised when he accepted my invitation.

The meeting was in a large tent. Bill, Mandela, and I were asked to sit on the stage and make brief comments. Conveners of the session had asked us not to defy or criticize President Mbeki's policies but simply to express our hope that the raging epidemic might be controlled. The event was well publicized. Television stations broadcast our remarks and newspapers carried a photograph of the three of us holding babies and their mothers, who had AIDS, sitting in the front row. Bill was feeding his crying baby with a bottle.

That night and the next morning the publicity was enormous in South Africa, because it was the first time Mandela had expressed approval for the treatment of AIDS with Western medicines; Mbeki had not even acknowledged the need for an aggressive response to the devastating impact of AIDS in their country, where the rate of infection had grown in the previous twelve years from less than 1 percent to more than 20 percent of all adults, with an estimated 1,800 new people being infected each day. There were predictions that 7 million already infected people would die in the next eight years. Some leaders of minor political groups had been attacking the African National Congress leaders for their refusal to confront the problem.

Bill and I met with groups of sex workers in brothels who volunteered to discuss how they became prostitutes, their special problems, family affairs when not "on duty," and awareness of their possible role in the spreading of AIDS to transient workers and others who would carry the infection to their wives and families back home. The women said there were about five thousand sex workers in the community but they were acquainted with only a small number of them. Even those who had been introduced to the trade involuntarily by being sold by their parents or others let us know that they now continued their work on their own volition. We found small groups of women who told us that they insisted on their customers using condoms, but this restraint commanded lower fees and was not appreciated by the brothel's supervisors. All of them denied having any symptoms of AIDS and seemed to have a fatalistic attitude toward their chances in the future. It was obvious that their customers were aware of the threat of AIDS and often expressed a preference for younger girls, who they believed were more likely to be free of the infection. Unlike in most other African countries, Rosalynn and I never saw an anti-AIDS poster or billboard in South Africa.

We flew to Capetown to meet with President Mbeki and found him waiting for us with his minister of health, Manto Tshabalala-Msimang. As Bill and I began to explain the purpose of our visit, the president interrupted and insisted that there was no scientific connection between HIV infection and AIDS and that the antiretroviral medicines we were promoting were toxic. The discussion became heated, and he and I rose from our chairs and faced each other in an angry confrontation. Mbeki accused us of attempting to introduce Western medicines into Africa to interfere with the progress being made by black people in eliminating the last vestiges of colonialism, and he claimed that President Robert Mugabe of Zimbabwe was also aware of our plot. We left South Africa without reconciling our differences, but since then I have worked harmoniously with President Mbeki in trying to bring peace to the people of Sudan.

We next visited Namibia (with a 23 percent infection rate), Angola (8 percent), and Nigeria (5.8 percent). President Olusegun Obasanjo brought representatives from all thirty-two Nigerian states to Abuja, where we had a discussion about the incidence of AIDS in different regions. When Bill and I visited with commercial sex workers, one group in the ghetto area of Mabushi, who were especially young and beautiful, told us they demanded that their clients use condoms. Some reported being offered five times their standard rate for "naked sex." Few of the other five thousand sex workers took any precautions against AIDS.

On Saturday afternoon President Obasanjo informed me that the next day there would be a Baptist religious service in the presidential chapel and that I was scheduled to deliver a sermon—about AIDS! I gave a lot of thought to the subject that night and decided that the best approach was to make it easy and acceptable for both men and women to report their infection by minimizing the stigma involved. I tried to explain to the large and emotional congregation how Jesus would address the problem of illicit sex, contagion, and suffering. I quoted texts about his attitude toward Mary Magdalene (who was cured of seven sins), the Samaritan woman at the well (with five lovers), and the woman caught in adultery and sentenced to be stoned to death. I said that all these actions showed his love and forgiveness and that Matthew 25's "unto the least of these" put the responsibility on all of us to reach out to the afflicted with forgiveness and love. President Obasanjo complimented me on my choice of biblical references and said that the congregation responded well.

We made a last-minute decision to stop in Bangui, Central African Republic, one of the most isolated and poverty-stricken countries in the world. We visited their only AIDS clinic, and it was a heartrending experience. There was a line of 267 people with AIDS, mostly mothers holding emaciated babies, but there was no medicine available. They were waiting for the daily allowance of a morsel of food. When the women were no longer able to walk, they were moved to the nearby hospital to die. Ninety percent of the hospital beds were filled with these patients. There was a young Japanese woman running the clinic, whose dedication reminded us of Mother Teresa, and Bill promised the Gates Foundation would provide special help to her and her patients.

In Kenya, President Daniel arap Moi was deeply involved in the AIDS issue and able to report a recent decrease in the national infection rate to 13 percent, although 20 percent of the citizens of Nairobi were infected. He joined us in a large public discussion on HIV/AIDS, where we heard vivid testimony from AIDS victims, commercial sex workers, AIDS orphans, students, workers, employers, and officials in the nation's AIDS programs.

We knew at that time that 35 percent of the citizens of Botswana were HIV-positive, and later the Gates Foundation joined with Merck & Co., a major producer of antiretroviral medicines, to concentrate on Botswana, with an emphasis on both prevention and treatment, to set an example for the rest of Africa.

With increased financial assistance from the President's Emergency Plan For AIDS Relief (PEPFAR), the U.S. government program promoted by President George W. Bush, improved education programs, and support from President Mbeki's successors and other political leaders, there has been dramatic progress in Africa. Eight times as many people are now receiving antiretroviral treatment, deaths from AIDS have been reduced by one-third, and new HIV infections are 25 percent lower than in 2002.

One of the setbacks in Africa has been in Uganda, which had a superb anti-AIDS program when we were on this trip. By using the standard "ABC" program (abstinence, be faithful, and condoms) the HIV/AIDS rate had dropped from more than 15 percent to 6 percent and was continuing its decline. In addition to teaching the ABC approach in schools, the Ugandan government conducted an aggressive media campaign using print, billboards, radio, and television. However, shortly after our trip, the president's wife was convinced by conservative Christian leaders in America to restrict the use of condoms, and the government shifted to promoting abstinence as the sole means of controlling the spread of AIDS. The result has been a lack of further progress in reducing the rates of death and new cases. Human Rights Watch has commented that the change in policy "leave[s] Uganda's children at risk of HIV," which is disputed, of course, by some of the faith-based groups. A report by the Joint United Nations Program on HIV/AIDS on Uganda in 2012 stated, "The number of newly infected people per year has increased by over 50 percent, from 99,000 in 2001 to 150,000 in 2011."

Most transmission of AIDS in Africa is through heterosexual activity. Women are less able to protect themselves from unwanted sex, and are most willing to implement the restraints of abstinence and the use of condoms. Except for professional sex workers, women are also less likely than men to transmit HIV/AIDS into a previously healthy home. Pregnant women are also eager, if infected, to protect their babies with antiretroviral medication. Protection of women from rape and providing them with preventive instruction and treatment should be priorities in the war against AIDS.

13 | SPOUSE ABUSE

A very difficult Christian text for battered women is Matthew 5:39, "If anyone slaps you on the right cheek, turn to them the other cheek also." This text is invoked to convince battered women it is "Christian" to just take abuse, and it is a very difficult text for them. But theologian Walter Wink, in his book *Engaging the Powers*, shows us the real meaning of that text in Jesus' time was nonviolent resistance. Jesus rejected the two common ways of responding to being treated violently, either violent resistance or passive acceptance. Instead, Jesus advocated a third way, that is, an assertive but nonviolent response when understood in the context of how Romans treated Jews in ancient Israel. A woman who is being beaten can choose the third way of active, but nonviolent resistance, by going to a battered women's shelter. That was the real meaning of Jesus' teaching.

REV. DR. SUSAN BROOKS THISTLETHWAITE,

PROFESSOR OF THEOLOGY AND FORMER PRESIDENT,

CHICAGO THEOLOGICAL SEMINARY

The World Health Organization reported in 2013 that more than a third of all women are victims of physical or sexual violence and that the vast majority are attacked or abused by their husbands or boyfriends. To some degree, this situation is perpetuated by local custom or helpless acquiescence by the abused women. About a third of countries do not have any laws against domestic violence, and many wives consider it mandatory and proper to submit themselves to their husbands for punishment. A recent UNICEF survey among women ages fifteen to forty-nine revealed that 90 percent of wives in Afghanistan and Jordan, 87 percent in Mali, 86 percent in Guinea and Timor-Leste, 81 percent in Laos, and 80 percent in Central African Republic believe that a husband is justified in hitting or beating his wife under certain circumstances.

At some time in their lives, one-fourth of all American women are victims of domestic violence. The Federal Bureau of Investigation reports that while 3,200 servicemen were killed in battle between 2000 and 2006, there were 10,600 domestic homicides in the United States; 85 percent of these victims were women. Since reports of such crimes by local police are discretionary, these data are an underestimation. The usual way of preventing these crimes has been to send battered women to protective shelters, but this has been only partially effective and imposes punishment on the victim instead of the attacker, especially when women have to leave children behind or take them into extended hiding.

A *New Yorker* magazine article by Rachel Louise Snyder in July 2013 describes a new approach that was initiated in Massachusetts in 2005, designed to prevent domestic homicide by using existing legal means to anticipate when it might happen. The most persistent predictor of these crimes was a prior incident of physical abuse: half of the female murder victims had earlier sought protection from the police. Although poverty of the family did not indicate likely violence, chronic unemployment of the husband was significant. Legal restraining orders on the abuser's movements had often been violated, but the combination of a "dangerousness" assessment and a court-ordered GPS locator on the abuser proved to be remarkably effective. Since the new program was put into effect there has not been a homicide in the test area and none of the offenders monitored by GPS has committed an act of domestic violence. In the most recent report, only 5 percent have had to go into a shelter for protection, while 90 percent would have done so before the new system was established. Thirty-three states have introduced or already passed laws to permit the use of the GPS restraint in domestic violence cases, and more than five thousand people from thirty states have been trained to implement this surprisingly inexpensive system.

Another rapidly expanding approach to reducing extreme cases of spouse abuse was described in *Bloomberg Businessweek* in September 2013: letting women in the developing world obtain a divorce from an abusive husband. The divorce rate has almost tripled since 1980 in Mexico, and there has been more than a fivefold increase in China, Iran, Thailand, and South Korea. Analysts attribute this increased freedom of women to make decisions with the implementation of the UN's Convention on the Elimination of All Forms of Discrimination Against Women. Simply put, many abused wives have been able to obtain a legal right to leave a troubled marriage permanently. Major challenges still remain, as rape within marriage is not a crime in 127 countries.

Ending violence against women requires advocacy to blossom into engaged global support by both leaders and community members. Each of us will be held accountable by God to take a stand against all forms of injustice in both private and public spheres. Preventive domestic violence education and training of religious leaders and communities must be institutionalized through sermons, premarital counseling, marital seminars, awareness campaigns, signed declarations, resource development, research, and survivor programs and services. We human beings all want the same thing—love and peace. Collectively we can create a world where we put into practice the universal principle of wanting for others what we want for ourselves—to best sustain peaceful families, communities, and nations.

IMAM MOHAMED MAGID, PRESIDENT,
ISLAMIC SOCIETY OF NORTH AMERICA, AND
MAHA B. ALKHATEEB, CODIRECTOR OF PR AND
RESEARCH, PEACEFUL FAMILIES PROJECT

We have all heard about the extreme derogation of women and girls in Afghanistan in regions controlled by the Taliban, and I have been involved personally in one perhaps illustrative case. Even when a girl is able to obtain a good education and escape a forced marriage at an early age, she is still not free to shape the rest of her life in a culture that supports male domination.

One of my best friends is Mashuq Askerzada, a former Muslim army officer from Afghanistan, who came to nearby Fort Benning, Georgia, for advanced military training after an earlier education at the Royal Military Academy Sandhurst in England. When Soviet troops invaded Afghanistan in December 1979, Mashuq decided to remain in America, married and had a family, and became a high school teacher. He attended my Bible class in Plains and became a Christian, and his family moved to our town to live. They are members of our church, and Mashuq teaches when I'm not there. (Some regular church members have been heard to say that they're glad when I'm away.)

Mashuq retained close contact with his relatives in Afghanistan and was especially proud of a young relative named Khatera. She had completed high school and two years of college and was preparing to become a teacher in one of the few institutes girls were permitted to attend. The family was relatively affluent and influential, and were greatly embarrassed and distressed early in 2007 when her father was arrested and falsely charged by the local judge with involvement in the misdeeds of his former business partners.

Two months later Khatera answered the telephone one day in their home and was surprised when the caller identified himself as the judge, who informed her that he had total power over her father and then violated sensitive cultural norms by saying he had heard that she was very beautiful and also well educated. She expressed her dismay and said she would hand the telephone to her mother, who had received an earlier demand from the judge for a payment of $10,000 for her husband's freedom and had already paid him $4,000. The judge told Khatera that if she informed her mother of his call, her father would never be released and it was very likely that her seventeen-year-old brother would be killed. He added that he would guarantee the family's safety and the father's freedom if Khatera would marry him. He told her he was a young bachelor and would provide her with a good life.

Her mother found her weeping in her room, but she decided not to tell anyone about the threats and promises. Later that week two trucks loaded with armed militia came to the house and surrounded it. The judge's sister entered and repeated her brother's offer to Khatera's mother, who was shocked and angry. In the meantime, in order to protect her family, the young woman had decided to accept the offer of marriage.

Three days later the judge arrived, accompanied by a mullah who read the proper religious words in the presence of the mother. Then the judge was permitted to approach Khatera, who was completely veiled. She saw that he was at least twenty-five years older than he had led her to expect. On the wedding night the husband brandished a large knife and said he would cut her into bits if she was not found to be a virgin.

Khatera bled as expected and was informed the next day that her father had been released from prison. That was when she met the judge's two other wives, one of whom was put in charge of her. When Khatera's mother learned of his former marriages, she berated the judge, after which he beat her daughter severely and repeatedly, warning her never again to share any information with her family. She was put on starvation rations and was soon notified by the other wives that their husband was searching for a fourth. Although Khatera did not complain, her mother was aware of her plight and told her that the judge had put her father back in prison. Khatera learned that she was up for sale when she was forced to unveil herself and greet two strange men, whom the judge identified as his "friends." A daughter of the judge later told her that she had heard them bargaining about the price to be paid. A few weeks later Khatera's mother induced the judge to permit her daughter to attend a wedding for another member of their family. Khatera was accompanied by members of the judge's militia and was taken back to her husband's home after the ceremony. Her mother appealed to the local governor and other officials, but they all sided with the judge, who accused the mother of trying to kidnap her daughter.

This was when Mashuq informed me about his family's problems. Some of his acquaintances in Afghanistan appealed to a high official who was from the same community. There was a temporary stalemate, and Khatera was escorted to a United Nations office in Kundu. When the judge went there with ten of his militia and threatened to burn down the office, the terrified staff members called a distant relative of the Askerzadas who was living nearby and who took Khatera to a UN office in the capital city, Kabul. I first interceded by telephone to outline the history of the case to the U.S. ambassador and offered to call the White House and the UN secretary-general. Khatera was transferred to a women's shelter in a secret location, which she later described as a prison.

I knew Burhanuddin Rabbani, who had served as president of Afghanistan for a brief time late in 2001, and he and I were able to obtain some influential help in Jalalabad, the judge's hometown. I wanted Khatera to come to America, but she was still officially married and there was no way we could overcome the multiple legal impediments. Although he and Khatera never saw each other again, her husband was induced to make a public declaration in the presence of officials that he was divorcing her and pledge never again to harm her or her family. He was suspended from his duties and later was shot in a Taliban attack and lost both legs. (President Rabbani was killed in 2011 in a suicide bombing.)

Khatera's journey to a normal life began when she resumed teaching in a girls' school in Afghanistan for two years and served as principal for a year. But then her school was bombed in a Taliban attack. Threatened that she would be cut to pieces if she returned to work, Khatera moved with her mother and youngest brother to Tajikistan. At that point Mashuq's son, William, realized that the only way to cut through most of the bureaucracy was to marry Khatera. He went to Tajikistan to meet her and, to his surprise, they fell deeply in love. William returned to America to file a petition for his fiancée to join him. I helped expedite the visa process, and after a few months Khatera was reunited with William and joined her relatives in Plains. Khatera and William were married and now have a handsome young son named for his father.

The significance of this story is that the drama of a beautiful and intelligent young woman would have had an entirely different ending if her family had not been able to depend on a former president of the United States and a former president of Afghanistan—and her cousin—for help. Few other women have such resources.

The need to secure women's rights, as a notion that is both Islamic and Afghan, is imperative in order for Afghanistan to be able to safeguard women's rights in the long term, particularly as security is transferred to domestic forces. In this traditional society where Islam shapes culture, traditions, and customs, there is no better way to raise the sensitive topic of women's rights than through community-level religious leaders themselves. Although we can help to facilitate these conversations, it is the Imams who share the message of women's rights according to Islam in a direct but non-threatening manner to a wider population—something that needs to happen more often.

PALWASHA KAKAR, DIRECTOR OF WOMEN'S
EMPOWERMENT AND DEVELOPMENT PROGRAMS,
THE ASIA FOUNDATION

14 | "HONOR" KILLINGS

Although widely condemned in the modern world, the terrible custom of "honor" killings is either legal or not prosecuted in some countries. It has a justification in the ancient Holy Scriptures of Jews and Christians. I remember when, during my first year in the White House, a Saudi couple who were living together were executed publicly; their desire to be married was rejected by her father. A British journalist researched the story and developed it into a film entitled *Death of a Princess*. Saudi government officials complained strenuously when the dramatized documentary was shown in Great Britain and were unable to prevent its showing by the Public Broadcasting System in the United States despite pressure from an oil company that was a major PBS sponsor.

This was the first time I became aware of the special laws and customs relating to the extreme consequences of a woman having sex outside of an approved marriage, but I was aware of a passage in the Holy Bible that espoused this ultimate punishment. In Deuteronomy 22:13–14, 20–21 we read, "If a man takes a wife and after lying with her dislikes her, and slanders her and gives her a bad name, saying, 'I married this woman, but when I approached her I did not find proof of her virginity,' . . . if the charge is true and no proof of the girl's virginity can be found, she shall be brought to the door of her father's house and there the men of her town shall stone her to death. . . . You must purge the evil from among you."

It is hard to believe that there is still a prevailing custom in many communities to murder a woman who has been raped, refuses to accept an assigned husband, has an extramarital affair, or even wears inappropriate clothing. This is done in order to salvage the honor of the besmirched family. It is difficult to obtain accurate data on how widespread this practice may be, because many of the killings are reported as suicides. They occur most frequently in the Middle East and South Asia, but also in other regions of the world. In 2010 the police reported 2,823 honor attacks in the United Kingdom. A BBC report estimates that globally more than twenty thousand women are victims of honor killings each year. There was a highly publicized case in Pakistan in 1999 of a mentally retarded girl whose rapist was identified and arrested. She was killed by a group of her tribesmen who claimed she had brought shame to the tribe. She was sixteen years old. Such murders are usually carried out by the girl's father, uncle, or younger brother.

The right to life of women in Pakistan is conditional on their obeying social norms and traditions.

HINA JILANI, PAKISTANI HUMAN RIGHTS

ACTIVIST AND AN ELDER

Human Rights Watch defines honor killings as "acts of vengeance, usually death, committed by male family members against female family members, who are held to have brought dishonor upon the family. A woman can be targeted by individuals within her family for a variety of reasons, including: refusing to enter into an arranged marriage, being the victim of a sexual assault, seeking a divorce—even from an abusive husband—or for allegedly committing adultery. The mere perception that a woman has behaved in a way that 'dishonors' her family is sufficient to trigger an attack on her life."

This definition does not include the killing of girls because their dowry is inadequate, but it applies to those who object to marriage because they believe they are too young or prefer a different husband than the one chosen by their parents. It is a custom, all too widely accepted, that derives from the belief that girls and women are the property of the males in their family.

There are some pressures from the global community to end the custom of honor killing, but these are having mixed results. King Abdullah II of Jordan and his wife, Rania, have attempted to end the legal practice, but their best efforts have been thwarted by strong community beliefs. The previous law stated, "He who discovers his wife or one of his female relatives committing adultery and kills, wounds or injures one or both of them, is exempt from any penalty." Stricter legislation concerning murder has been passed, but courts can commute or reduce sentences in honor killings, particularly if the victim's family (who are usually the culprits) asks for leniency. In many cases, the custom is to let the crime be committed by a brother who is less than eighteen years old, that is, a juvenile, so that any punishment will be quite minor.

Just an allegation is often adequate to condemn the girl, without any proof of improper conduct. The director of Jordan's National Institute of Forensic Medicine has found the hymens intact in a number of postmortem examinations of victims of honor killings. A recent study by researchers from Cambridge University stated, "While stricter legislation has been introduced—despite conservative fears—cultural support for violence against women who are seen as breaking norms has remained widespread." The university's Institute of Criminology found that almost 50 percent of boys and 20 percent of girls interviewed in the capital, Amman, believe that killing a daughter, sister, or wife who has "dishonored" or shamed the family is justified.

Tragically the practice is still all too prevalent in the Islamic world. Egypt's interior minister reported in 2000 that 16 percent of homicides were family killings to "wipe out shame." Between 2002 and 2003 the Egyptian Association of Legal Aid for Women reported that perpetrators of violence were husbands, fathers, brothers, and uncles in 75 percent of the cases; women represented the other 25 percent. It is almost impossible for a rape victim to prove her innocence, because she must have four adult male Muslim eyewitnesses testify on her behalf. Such killings have also been committed in Hindu and Sikh communities in India, and by Christians within highly patriarchal cultures.

15 | GENITAL CUTTING

One of the most serious and least understood examples of abuse of girls is the removal of all or part of their genitalia. Known as female genital cutting or female circumcision, the operation is usually performed without anesthesia, with a knife or razor blade by women who are known as "cutters." Some cutters use sutures to close the wound, leaving a small hole for the girl to pass urine and menstrual blood. At the time of marriage or childbirth, the hole is enlarged enough to accommodate the husband's penis or the infant.

FGC can result in lifelong health consequences, including chronic infection; severe pain during urination, menstruation, sexual intercourse, and childbirth; and psychological trauma. Some girls die from the cutting, usually as a result of bleeding or infection.

The World Health Organization estimates that about 125 million women and girls have undergone FGC, ostensibly to "purify" them by reducing their enjoyment of or desire for sex. Some practitioners claim that female genitalia are dirty and should be made flat, rigid, and dry. In many communities the operation is considered to be the passage of girls into womanhood, although it is most often performed at a very young age. Some believe that it helps to enhance men's enjoyment of the sex act. There are no Holy Scriptures that mandate the practice, but some Christians, Jews, Muslims, animists, and nature worshipers have adopted FGC as part of their local religious teaching.

The subject of female genital cutting was discussed at the World Conference on Human Rights in Vienna in 1993 and declared to be a serious abuse of small girls. Since then almost all countries have passed laws that forbid or restrict the practice, and in December 2012 the United Nations General Assembly unanimously passed a resolution banning the practice. However, these international and national resolutions and laws have had practically no effect in restricting the abuse, and legal punishment is almost nonexistent.

The resistance to outside interference and the need for local people to make their own decisions have been most vividly demonstrated in Senegal by the work of Tostan, founded by Molly Melching, who was a student at the University of Dakar in 1974 and later an exchange student and a U.S. Peace Corps Volunteer. She settled in a village of three hundred people in the eastern region of the country and became assimilated into the local society. She used her good education to teach the women how to read and write, about the outside world, and how to care for themselves and their family's health. Perhaps more important, she taught women that they had basic human rights, of which they had previously been unaware. Molly recognized that the Senegalese women, and not outsiders, had to be the ones to make decisions about their own lives, and she developed a system of community empowerment that later adopted the name Tostan, or "empowerment." Molly emphasizes that 99 percent of the Tostan staff are Senegalese.

The practice of female genital cutting was accepted without question in many Senegalese villages, along with the assumption that the status of women was inherently inferior to that of men. In 1997 one group of women decided to abandon the practice in their community, based on the new understanding that it was harmful to their health and a violation of their human rights. They also learned from the words of respected Muslim leaders that it had no basis in the teachings of the Koran. Village by village, this awareness has spread throughout many Senegalese regions where the practice is traditional, and as of 2013 women in more than 6,400 villages, primarily in Senegal but also in Guinea, The Gambia, Mauritania, Djibouti, and Somalia, have decided to abandon the practice of genital cutting and also the forced marriage of children. Molly states that the key factor in this achievement by African women was informing them about the universal agreements concerning the rights of women and then letting them make the decision for themselves.

A report issued by UNICEF in July 2013 showed a very gradual reduction in genital cutting but emphasized that it was still overwhelmingly prevalent in some countries, especially those in Africa where the Islamic faith prevails. UNICEF estimates that 91 percent of women in Egypt, 98 percent in Somalia, 96 percent in Guinea, 93 percent in Djibouti, 89 percent in Eritrea, 89 percent in Mali, 88 percent in Sierra Leone, and 88 percent in Sudan have undergone some form of genital cutting, and more than 50 percent of the women in Burkina Faso, Chad, Ethiopia, The Gambia, Guinea-Bissau, and Kenya have also been cut.

There have been surprising reductions in Kenya and Central African Republic. It is not clear why this is so, but it seems obvious that outside pressure has had little effect except in encouraging the education of young women. For instance a 2008 report in Egypt showed that although 81 percent of fifteen- to nineteen-year-old women had been cut, 96 percent of women in their late forties had been subjected to the procedure—evidence of a slight but significant reduction among the younger generation. A public opinion poll that same year revealed that only a third of the younger women wanted to see the practice continue, while two-thirds of the older women supported its continuation. Because the decision to perform FGC is made almost exclusively by mothers, without consulting their husbands, these numbers give hope that the next generation of daughters might be spared. Another hopeful trend observed in several countries was that the more severe forms of genital cutting were less prevalent among younger women.

Although UNICEF found little evidence of progress in Senegal, the researchers explained that their survey did not include the area where Tostan has been most active; in addition, they surveyed women age fifteen to nineteen, while in Senegal 75 percent of girls are cut between birth and age four. In fact, UNICEF was confident that the Tostan effect would prevail in the future.

This is an extremely sensitive subject, especially when criticism of the practice comes from "outsiders" who are suspected of wanting to change the cultural, religious, and sometimes political heritage of the local people. Nevertheless, this abuse of girls is too serious and too important to be ignored or accepted by national governments where it exists or by the UN and other international organizations. Local efforts like Tostan should be supported and replicated to ensure sustained eradication of such harmful practices.

16 | CHILD MARRIAGE AND DOWRY DEATHS

Another serious and pervasive example of gender abuse is the marriage of young girls, often without their consent and contrary to their best interests. There are an estimated 14 million girls married every year before they reach the age of eighteen, and 1 in 9 of these are younger than fifteen. This includes 48 percent of young brides in South Asia; 42 percent in Sub-Saharan Africa; 29 percent in Latin America and the Caribbean; and 18 percent in the Middle East and North Africa. Girls from poor families are nearly twice as likely to be married at an early age as girls from wealthier families. This is a traditional practice in many societies, primarily because girls are not considered equal in value to boys and are often believed to be a burden to their family. When poverty is a factor, marrying off a daughter is a convenient way to eliminate the need to feed her. Another financial incentive is the "bride price" paid to the girl's family.

A traditional practice that has become subject to serious abuse is the payment of a dowry by the bride's family. Especially in India and Pakistan and their neighbors it has become more prevalent in recent years, and the amount paid has also increased. Recognizing this bur-

den, especially on poor families, India and other countries have out-
lawed the practice, but the law is widely ignored, even among the more
affluent families. Since girls are considered to be a burden on the family
and unmarried ones an embarrassment, many families are willing to go
bankrupt to get them married. As a result, thousands of young women
suffer. In January 2012, the *Times of India* reported an increase in the
killing of brides by greedy husbands and in-laws when they don't receive enough money and jewelry from the bride's parents, or in lieu of
returning unsatisfactory brides (along with the dowry) to their parents.
This terrible crime is called "dowry death," and women's organizations
in India have increased pressure for more stringent laws against it. In
1986 a law was passed against murder resulting from harassment for
dowry, with a section added later to define more specifically the crimes
of harassment and cruelty by the husbands and their families. However,
these stricter laws have had little effect: when cases are actually brought
to trial, conviction rates have dropped. In 2000, 6,995 dowry deaths
were reported under these new laws; in 2010, 94,000 cases were reported, with a conviction rate of just 19 percent; in 2012 the number of
cases fell to 8,233. There is no data yet available for the conviction rate.

There are proven disadvantages for child brides concerning their
health, education, safety, and loss of the basic human right of making decisions about their own lives. Young brides under fifteen are five
times more likely to die in childbirth than women in their twenties,
and when a woman is under eighteen her baby is 60 percent more likely
to die in its first year of life than a baby born to a woman just two years
older. Few child brides are permitted to remain in school, which de-
prives them of the ability to support themselves or a family. In addition,
they are more likely to suffer domestic violence and sexual abuse. All
these statistics are derived from publications of United Nations agencies. This mistreatment contravenes both the Convention on the Rights
of the Child and the Convention on the Elimination of All Forms of
Discrimination Against Women.

If the abuses of child marriage continue at the present rate, then about 15 million girls will be added each year to the list of victims. This terrible situation has been ignored by most of the international community, largely because the young girls are inarticulate, their families have a selfish financial interest, and political leaders consider the prohibition of forced child marriage a taboo issue since it is supported by traditional and religious culture.

I am a member of The Elders, a group of former political leaders, peace activists, and human rights advocates who were brought together by Nelson Mandela in 2007. The goal Mandela set for us was to use our "almost 1,000 years of collective experience" to work on solutions for problems involving peace, human rights, climate change, and disease. One of the criteria we adopted is to be free of political pressures by not holding public office, but all of us have had experience in high positions.*

The Elders have been active in attempts to promote peace and human rights in the Middle East, Sudan and South Sudan, North and South Korea, Zimbabwe, Cyprus, Kenya, Egypt, and Myanmar and in addressing the impending disaster of global warming. But one of our most challenging and exciting commitments has been to promote equality for women and girls.

We had an extensive debate when I presented my concerns about the adverse impact of religious beliefs on women's rights to this group of fellow leaders and advisors in 2008, because they represent practicing Protestants, Catholics, Jews, Muslims, and Hindus, and their faiths

*The Elders are Martti Ahtisaari, president of Finland, Nobel Peace laureate; Kofi Annan, secretary-general of the United Nations, Nobel Peace laureate; Ela Bhatt, founder of the Self-Employed Women's Association of India; Lakhdar Brahimi, foreign minister of Algeria and United Nations envoy; Gro Harlem Brundtland, prime minister of Norway and director-general of the World Health Organization; Fernando Henrique Cardoso, president of Brazil; Jimmy Carter, president of the United States, Nobel Peace laureate; Hina Jilani, Pakistani lawyer and UN special representative on human rights defenders; Graça Machel, education minister of Mozambique and widow of Nelson Mandela; Mary Robinson, president of Ireland and United Nations high commissioner for human rights; and Ernesto Zedillo, president of Mexico.

have different policies about the status of women. We finally decided to draw particular attention to the role of religious and traditional leaders in obstructing the campaign for equality and human rights and promulgated the following statement: "The justification of discrimination against women and girls on grounds of religion or tradition, as if it were prescribed by a Higher Authority, is unacceptable. Having served as local, state, national, and world leaders, we understand why many public officials can be reluctant to question ancient religious and traditional premises—an arena of great power and sensitivity. We are calling on all those with influence to challenge and change the harmful teachings and practices—in religious and secular life—that justify discrimination against women, and to acknowledge and emphasize the positive messages of equality and human dignity."

After The Elders agreed to adopt the eradication of gender abuse as a priority project in 2008, it soon became obvious that the greatest opportunity for our group to make a direct and immediate contribution was by concentrating on child marriage. The Elders formed a global partnership with about three hundred nongovernmental organizations from more than fifty countries that share the commitment to end child marriage. We named this coalition Girls Not Brides, and it grew to such an extent that it was separated into an independent organization in 2013, with The Elders still fully supportive of its goals. All the NGO partners are continuing work in their own areas, and substantial progress is being made in raising international concern about the issue. Plans have been announced to raise the subject with the UN Human Rights Council, with the hope of reaching a General Assembly resolution condemning the practice.

In the meantime other action is being taken. In 2013 Human Rights Watch released a ninety-five-page report on South Sudan that documents the near total lack of protection for girls and women who try to resist marriage or leave abusive marriages and the obstacles they face in achieving any relief from their plight. The U.S. Congress has passed a law that requires the inclusion of child marriage in its annual Human

Rights Report and mandates that the secretary of state develop a strategy to prevent child marriage, including diplomatic and program initiatives. Both the United Nations and the World Bank have announced commitments to publicize the problem and to induce nations to end the practice.

There are many encouraging developments; one is a special effort to assess the links between child marriage and slavery and to sharpen national and local laws so they are more specific and punitive when girls are forced to act against their will. Despite the persistence of the practice in many communities, these efforts have had some tangible benefits. In ninety-two countries surveyed in 2005, 48 percent of women forty-five to forty-nine years old were married as children, but the proportion is only 35 percent for women who are now twenty to twenty-four. The trend is good news, but the number is still far too high!

17 | POLITICS, PAY, AND
MATERNAL HEALTH

On a global basis, women are habitually denied full and equal participation in political affairs, despite provision for it in the UN's Universal
Declaration of Human Rights. The United States has struggled with
the issue. The Fifteenth Amendment to the U.S. Constitution granted
black men the right to vote in 1870, ninety-four years after the declaration "All men are created equal." It was fifty years later that American women won the same constitutional status (though, with few
exceptions, only white women could enjoy this right in practice), and
slow progress was realized after that time. Franklin D. Roosevelt
was the first president to select a woman to occupy a cabinet post,
and other presidents and I have chosen women for major roles in our
cabinets and White House staff. I was able to appoint women to key
cabinet posts, and a growing number of women are now serving as
governors, in the House and Senate, and as chief executive officers
of major corporations. In nations as diverse as India, Pakistan, Indonesia, Israel, Great Britain, the Philippines, Liberia, and Nicaragua
women have served as presidents and prime ministers. These nations
represent citizens who are predominantly Hindu, Muslim, Jewish,

and Christian and include two of the three largest democracies on earth.

As University Distinguished Professor at Emory University, I lecture in all the divisions: arts and sciences, law, theology, medicine, nursing, public health, and business. I usually speak for about thirty minutes and then answer questions from the students (and sometimes the professors). One of the subjects that I cover frequently is human rights, often involving gender discrimination, and a "trick" question I ask is "When did women gain the right to vote in the United States?" Hands shoot up and someone always offers the standard reply: "With the passage of the Nineteenth Amendment to the U.S. Constitution in 1920." I point out that this amendment applied only to white women, and that it was with the Voting Rights Act of 1965 under President Lyndon Johnson that all black women gained this privilege. This makes the point that racial, religious, and gender discrimination are often interrelated.

Globally, women first won the right to vote early in the twentieth century, beginning with New Zealand, Australia, and the Scandinavian countries. The Arab nations were the last to grant this privilege, and Saudi Arabian women are still not permitted to vote. (There is a promise that this opportunity will come in 2015, but similar commitments in 2009 and 2011 were rescinded.) Only recently have women begun to make real progress in holding major office in the political world. At this time there are fourteen female heads of state, the best known being Angela Merkel of Germany, Dilma Rousseff of Brazil, Cristina Kirchner of Argentina, Ellen Johnson Sirleaf of Liberia, Park Geun-hye of South Korea, and Joyce Banda of Malawi. There are about 46,500 parliamentarians in the world, and women occupy 21 percent of the seats. Rwanda ranks first, with 64 percent; Cuba has 49 percent; the five Scandinavian countries average 42 percent; the parliaments in the Western Hemisphere have 25 percent, Europe 23 percent, Sub-Saharan Africa 25 percent (but Nigeria only 7 percent), Asia 19 percent, and the combined Arab states 16 percent. This is inadequate progress.

When I was elected president in 1976 there were only eighteen women in the U.S. Congress (about 3 percent), but the number has increased steadily to 102 elected in 2012. This amounts to only 18 percent of the total, far below the world average and leaving our nation ranked 78th in women's participation in government. In state and local government in America, seventy-three women now hold elected statewide positions, or 23 percent of the total, after a steady decrease from 28 percent, the high point, in 1993. In Los Angeles, a community of almost 10 million people, there is only one woman in the entire government, a position in the city council. She recently commented, "When I was in elementary school, there were five women on the city council."

As with racial discrimination, it is very difficult to change historical societal patterns even when there is a desire to do so. I experienced this problem as president in overcoming the exclusion of women from service in the federal district courts and the more senior appellate courts. When there is a vacancy, White House staff members usually consult with the U.S. senators from the state involved, then give the president a list of potential appointees; then the president's nomination for judge is submitted to the Senate for confirmation. Prior to my election, only eight women had been appointed to the federal bench, and I was determined to correct this inequity. By the end of my term, I had a chance to fill about 45 percent of the seats in the federal courts.

At that time the primary obstacle in nominating qualified women was the relatively few female graduates of law schools, and not many of those had acquired enough seniority to become leaders in law firms or deans in university law schools. Another persistent problem was that many senators had close friendships and political obligations to men who occupied those positions. There was even an argument between my White House staff members and the attorney general I appointed, who claimed that there were very few qualified women and minority candidates. There was also some blatant prejudice against women serving as judges, and a few senators were able, through "senatorial courtesy," to block my choices.

Despite these obstacles, I was successful in having the Senate confirm five times as many women as all my predecessors combined, and in addition was able greatly to increase the number of judges from minority groups. I was fortunate also to have 88 percent of my judicial nominees approved by the Senate. There has been an encouraging increase in the number of women judges chosen by my successors, and the total in the United States is now at about 25 percent, compared to a worldwide average of 27 percent. It is obvious that, even under the best of circumstances, women have not been able to reach their potential of equal participation in executive, legislative, or judicial affairs.

One of my most interesting and ultimately gratifying experiences with female candidates began in 1994 with the visit to our home of an Indonesian official who was seeking a site to build small airplanes he had designed that could be modified very quickly from hauling cargo to carrying passengers. B. J. Habibie was a superbly trained aeronautical engineer from Indonesia who had earned his advanced degrees in Germany and became famous as a designer of innovative machines. He was serving as minister of research and engineering in the government of Indonesia's president Suharto.

I extolled the advantages of Georgia as the best location for a factory, and we had a long and enjoyable conversation about his interesting career and his new life in the world of government. I described some of the work of The Carter Center, including our having initiated the process of monitoring elections under often difficult circumstances. He and I communicated with each other a few times afterward, and he eventually informed me that plans for the manufacturing plant had been abandoned. Later I read with some surprise that President Suharto had been placed under house arrest, accused of corruption; he had chosen the nonpolitical engineer to be his vice president. When Suharto was forced to resign, Habibie became president of the largest Islamic nation in the world, which had been governed by dictators for forty-one years.

A few weeks later I had a call from President Habibie asking if The Carter Center would consider leading a team to observe their first democratic election, and I agreed to do so. We had a crash course in the history and culture of Indonesia and soon learned that there were almost fifty political parties with candidates seeking five hundred seats in the Parliament and that two hundred more members would be added from the military, women, youth, and other groups. After being assembled as a body, the seven hundred parliamentarians would then choose a president, presumably from the party that had prevailed in the election.

Rosalynn and I went first to Bali, a beautiful vacation site and home of the leading woman candidate, Dyah Permata Megawati Setiawati Sukarnoputri, who was known as Megawati and was the daughter of Indonesia's first president, Sukarno. It was the custom to demonstrate support for a candidate by flying a small party banner from the top of a tall bamboo pole, and we noticed the overwhelming prevalence of Megawati's following, especially in the small villages and rural areas. Indonesia comprises about nineteen thousand islands spread over a broad area of the western Pacific Ocean, and our one hundred observers covered as many of the key voting areas as possible.

Although there were heated debates among the many candidates, the people were thrilled to have the chance to choose their own political leaders and were especially careful to comply with the law and election rules. Ninety percent of registered voters cast their ballots, there was an honest counting procedure, and Megawati's party prevailed with 36 percent of the vote. This was followed by Suharto and Habibie's ruling party, with 23 percent. Three others received about 10 percent each, and the rest of the votes were scattered among minor parties.

Most of our observers returned home after the votes were counted, but we left a small group to observe the convening of the Parliament and choosing of a president. Habibie withdrew from contention, and it was widely assumed that Megawati would be elected, but there was intense opposition from some of the more militant Islamists to a woman having the highest office, and the Parliament voted instead for Abdurrahman Wahid, known as Gus Dur, a religious leader who had been aligned earlier with Megawati in reformist efforts. Since Wahid's party had received only 10 percent of the popular vote and elective legislative seats, this decision was hotly condemned, and the Parliament compromised by electing Megawati as vice president. Over the months Wahid proved to be an inept administrator and was forced to resign in 2001. Megawati became the first female president of Indonesia and the fourth chief executive of a Muslim nation, after Pakistan, Turkey, and Bangladesh elected women leaders. Megawati and other party leaders invited The Carter Center back to observe the next election, in 2004, after the constitution was changed to permit direct election of the president, and the incumbent was defeated in a runoff.

It is interesting to note that an overwhelming majority of citizens in the world's three largest democracies have different religions: India (81 percent Hindu), the United States (76 percent Christian), and Indonesia (87 percent Muslim). Two of them have elected women as leaders of their government.

One of the most widespread and punitive examples of sexual discrimination is in compensation for work. As women have achieved higher education levels, slow but steady progress has been realized since I was president thirty years ago, when the disparity in pay between American men and women was 39 percent. Although women compose almost half the U.S. workforce and now earn more college and graduate degrees than men, government statistics show that full-time female workers still earn about 23 percent less than men. Over the past decade there has been little improvement: the U.S. Census Bureau reports that women's full-time annual earnings were 76 percent of men's in 2001 and 76.5 percent in 2012.

There is also a wide variation in pay equality among nations. The Organization for Economic Co-operation and Development, which includes thirty-one countries that are committed to democracy and an economic system of free enterprise, reports that the pay disparity against women varies from 4 percent in New Zealand to 37 percent in South Korea, with a global average of 18 percent. Even in the most advanced countries women are paid less than men for the same work.

The difference at the executive level is even greater. Recent statistics show that among Fortune 500 companies only twenty-one CEOs are women, and at this top executive level women received, on average, 42 percent less compensation than men. Interestingly, Catalyst, a nonprofit organization, found a 26 percent better return on investment among American corporations whose board membership was more than one-fifth female than among those with no women serving. Perhaps the presence of women injects a wider range of perspectives, enriching the decision-making process; or it may be that those corporations with a more flexible and innovative approach—factors in success—were the ones inclined to involve women at the top level of governance.

There is every indication that it is beneficial for a business to have women directly involved in its management, but this change is slow in coming. In its annual analysis of 235 large European companies, McKinsey & Company has found that, despite concerted efforts in some countries to increase the number of women at senior levels, progress has been very slow, with only a 6 percent increase during the past ten years. They concluded in 2012 that even "if improvement continues at the present rate, ten years from now women will have less than 20 percent of the seats on boards or executive committees." Among the companies they surveyed only 2 percent of the chief executive officers were women, only 9 percent were on executive committees, while 37 percent were among total employees at all levels.

When my fellow Elder, Gro Brundtland, was prime minister of Norway (1990–96), she led her Labor Party to adopt a rule requiring at least 40 percent of each sex represented on political committees and elected groups. She told me that at times there was a problem finding enough qualified men to reach the 40 percent mark. Later, in 2003, a law was passed in Norway that required all publicly traded companies to appoint women to at least 40 percent of their board membership or the company would be removed from the Oslo Stock Exchange. After ten years there are mixed opinions about its impact. A relatively small group of women now occupy many different board positions and have come to be known as "golden skirts." One of them is quoted in the *New York Times* as saying that "it hasn't had a ripple effect" in bringing more female success in positions of importance in business. The prevailing sentiment, however, is that the law has been helpful in boosting women toward equal standing in the overall society, and the director of the Institute for Social Research in Norway states that having more female directors has had "a slightly positive effect" on economic performance.

When I was a student at Plains High School, there were only two male classroom teachers, plus one who concentrated exclusively on educating boys like me as future farmers. I remember how different it was when I became a freshman in 1941 at Georgia Southwestern College, where most of our professors were men. A 2011 report from the American Association of University Professors (AAUP) states that even in 1974–75, thirty years after I was a college student, only 22 percent of the full-time professors were women; the rate increased during the next thirty-six years, but only to an average of 42 percent.

Even in the field of higher education, where female enrollment is quite high, the economic disparity for women still prevails. According to the AAUP report, the number of women exceeded 57 percent of both undergraduate and graduate students in American universities. However, they held just 28 percent of full professorships. Among current presidents of colleges and universities, 23 percent are women, the number having doubled during the past twenty-five years, but the overall pay gap was about the same as in general employment, with women's pay in full-time faculty positions about 80 percent of men's.

A 2013 study at Yale University showed that established professionals in science, technology, engineering, and mathematics (the STEM subjects) are much more willing to give a job to a young male scientist than a woman with the same qualifications. If they did hire the woman, her average annual salary was nearly $4,000 lower than the man's. It was striking to note that interviewed female scientists were at least as biased against hiring and paying women as their male counterparts.

On the other hand, it is encouraging that over the past forty years the proportion of women PhD recipients has increased in engineering from 0.2 to 22.5 percent, in the geosciences from 3 to 36.6 percent, and in the physical sciences from 3.7 to 27.9 percent. However, women still hold far fewer full professorships than do men. Although women held 62 percent of the PhDs in psychology in a recent year, they held only 19 percent of tenured positions.

In terms of geography and college major, there are substantial differences between male and female students in U.S. universities, with a wide variation among different regions. For instance, in 2005 there were 40 percent more women than men students in the Southeast, and 10 percent fewer in Utah. The following shows the percentage of women enrolled in different disciplines in that same year: arts and humanities, 53 percent; biology, 53 percent; business, 43 percent; education, 69 percent; engineering, 15 percent; physical sciences, 43 percent; social sciences, 66 percent; technical, 27 percent; and computer sciences, 22 percent. These disparities in choice of major study are the result of many factors, including family influence, personal choice, preference for particular professors, and bias in hiring, but academic discrimination in enrollment is not significant.

I remember from my childhood during the Great Depression the very real threat that a woman might die during or shortly after giving birth. At that time, the death rate due to complications from childbirth for all American women was more than 600 per 100,000 births, and black women died at a much higher rate. My mother worked with the African American midwives in our Archery community to improve their skills. It was not the custom for prospective mothers to go to a hospital unless they were known to have an abnormal pregnancy, but the more affluent families could afford to have a trained obstetrician come to supervise home deliveries. Mama was the operating room nurse at Wise Sanitarium in Plains, and the chief surgeon, Dr. Sam Wise, was eager to reduce the amount of time away from her duties. It happened that there was an empty room available; Mama occupied it, and I turned out to be the first American president born in a hospital.

With the advent of antibiotics and more sterile techniques during childbirth, the maternal death rate for all American women decreased dramatically, reaching its lowest point in 1987 at 7.2 deaths per 100,000 live births. But since then it has been creeping upward. Because of poverty and other causes, black women are three to four times more likely than white women to die during pregnancy and childbirth. When the Centers for Disease Control and Prevention began assessing the causes of maternal deaths in 1987, hemorrhage was blamed for more than one in four deaths. Now the causes have shifted to stroke and other diseases of the heart and blood vessels, with obesity an increasing cause of concern.

Women's bodies can be particularly vulnerable because of our responsibilities and our duties around pregnancy, birth, and childcare. So for me, knowing the needs of women and ensuring the rights of women to fair and equal access to healthcare is core to the work of bioethics. The free market argument, while it has worked out for some, clearly has failed to deliver a world of peace and justice. The voice of religion says there has to be areas of human life that are not subject to the justice of the market. Most of those areas are ones about love, one's family, the human body, where those aspects of human life can't be sold and can't be commoditized in ways that are fair, because they live outside the language of the exchange. And here we need language about hospitality, generosity, abundance, and love.

DR. LAURIE ZOLOTH, BIOETHICIST AND PRESIDENT
OF THE AMERICAN ACADEMY OF RELIGION

On a global basis, one of the most notable examples of discrimination against women is their comparative lack of access to adequate health care. According to the World Health Organization, the fourth leading cause of death for women worldwide is poor conditions at childbirth, exceeded only by HIV/AIDS, malaria, and tuberculosis. Some significant progress is being made in most areas, as overall health care improves. In 1980, my last year in office, there were 526,300 deaths of women worldwide while pregnant or during childbirth, and 287,000 in 2010, which was a 45 percent reduction. The United Nations Millennium Development Goals had called for a 75 percent reduction by 2015, a target that obviously will not be reached. In Sub-Saharan Africa the maternal death rate is actually increasing. Globally 99 percent of maternal deaths occur in poor developing countries. This dramatic difference in maternal care between rich and poor countries is demonstrated clearly by the maternal mortality rate (MMR), the number of mothers' deaths for each 100,000 births.

According to the most recent data published by the World Health Organization and UNICEF, the MMR world average is 210, ranging from 2 in Estonia to more than 1,000 in Chad and Somalia, and the MMR average for all of Sub-Saharan Africa is 500. The average rate in Scandinavian countries and Western Europe is less than 10, and in the United States is 21. This places America at the bottom among industrialized nations, despite spending more per average patient than any other. The highest total number of deaths occurred in India (56,000), with a rate of 200, and Nigeria (40,000), with a rate of 630. Not surprisingly, the risk of maternal mortality is highest for adolescent girls under fifteen. Aside from the death itself, the tragic consequences for surviving children are tremendous.

One nation that is making good progress in correcting this problem is Ethiopia, among the poorest countries on earth, which we began visiting in 1988, when the oppressive communist dictator Mengistu Haile Mariam was still in power. It is said that he had gained his authority over the populous nation by personally smothering Emperor Haile Selassie in his bed, and all Western nations had broken diplomatic relations with his regime. While observing one of our agriculture projects in Tanzania in 1989, I received an urgent request from the International Red Cross and UN High Commissioner for Refugees to go to Addis Ababa to negotiate some arrangement by which supplies could be delivered to the two large refugee camps in Ethiopia that sheltered people escaping the ravages of wars in neighboring Somalia and Sudan. After an argument between these agencies and Mengistu, he had forbidden their access to the camps, and Rosalynn and I made an appointment to meet with him. Almost immediately he accepted my proposal to let the two agencies deliver food, water, and medicine to the camps, provided his troops could supervise the process. I became interested in the country, and later became a friend of Meles Zinawe, a revolutionary from Tigray, who eventually overthrew Mengistu, forcing him into permanent exile in Zimbabwe.

Meles became prime minister after a series of elections and launched a number of projects to improve the lot of his people, especially in the rural areas. On one of my visits, he asked if The Carter Center might be willing to train health workers, and, as described in a previous chapter, we met this request with an emphasis on providing women throughout Ethiopia with skills in midwifery, because maternal deaths were extremely high there. These workers also help with other projects of our Center in Ethiopia, including the treatment and elimination of malaria, trachoma, Guinea worm, and river blindness. Still at a very low level of income per person, Ethiopia has benefited greatly from an enlightened prime minister, dedicated cabinet officers, and citizens who are determined to improve their own lives. We are now planning similar training programs for public health workers in Sudan and Nigeria.

In 2008 the International Monetary Fund described the speed of Ethiopia's progress as "fastest for a non–oil exporting country in Sub-Saharan Africa." Ethiopia was also ranked as the second most attractive African country for investors. Meles was given the Africa Political Leadership Award and donated the $200,000 to a foundation called Fre-Addis Ethiopia Women Fund, which was dedicated "to empower girls through providing educational opportunities" by giving support to needy and orphan rural girls to pursue their education.

Intensive work is in progress to establish the post-2015 Millennium Development Goals. When they are adopted by the UN there is little doubt that maternal health will remain one of the top priorities, still unreached. It is hoped that publicity about sexual discrimination in politics, economics, work, and education plus stronger and more persistent demands from women's organizations will help to minimize these abuses.

18 | THE ROAD TO PROGRESS

There is no religion that despises women. Hatred cannot
come from the heart of God. If there is hatred, its source
is not the Creator. Only humans have the capacity to see
and treat others as less than they truly are. It is our minds
and hearts that must change to release women, girls, men,
and boys from the bondage of gender-based limitations or
violence. That change is happening, right now in this very
moment, in thousands of homes, schools, synagogues, cha-
pels, mosques, and centers of power around the world. That
change is coming. Have faith. It will be here soon.

RITU SHARMA, COFOUNDER AND PRESIDENT,

WOMEN THRIVE WORLDWIDE

It is interesting and helpful to have a way to assess how different countries compare in achieving equal status between men and women and
to ascertain if they are making progress. The World Economic Forum

has performed this service with its Global Gender Gap Report for the past seven years. It "assesses countries on how well they are dividing their resources and opportunities among their male and female populations, regardless of the overall levels of these resources and opportunities." The four primary criteria used in these assessments are (1) economic participation and opportunity (salary level and skilled employment); (2) educational attainment (access to basic and higher education); (3) political empowerment (involvement in decision making); and (4) health and survival (life expectancy and sex ratio of surviving children).

A score of 1.000 would indicate that women and men are treated with absolute equality. Iceland has the highest score, .8731, and other Scandinavian countries plus Switzerland, Ireland, New Zealand, the Philippines, and Nicaragua are in the top ten, all with scores above .7700. Other rankings and scores of interest are for Cuba (which ranks nineteenth, with a score of .7540), the United States (twenty-third, with .7382), Israel (fifty-third, with .7032), and Bangladesh (the highest ranked Islamic country at seventy-fifth, with .6848). The entire report can be found on the Internet. The individual factors indicate that the United States lags behind in wage equality at sixty-seventh and in numbers of women in political office at sixtieth.

The reports cover the status of gender equality in 136 countries, and since women comprise approximately half a nation's talent base, there is usually a direct relation between their treatment and their homeland's economic status. As expected, most of the Arab nations and those in Sub-Saharan Africa rank quite low. The general conclusion is that during the seven years of assessment the majority of countries have made very slow progress on closing the gender gap. For instance, the United States improved from .7042 in 2006, an increase of about 5 percent in seven years, but during the past year dropped from twenty-second to twenty-third in the global ranks.

One tremendous untapped resource in the global move to enhance women's rights is the private but formidable influence of first ladies and other prominent women who don't hold elective office. Let me give a few examples with which I am familiar. In the United States the most vivid illustration of this point has been Eleanor Roosevelt, who was a courageous spokesperson for black people while her husband was president, long before there was a detectable civil rights movement. I remember that she was despised by many in the Southland, even while FDR was winning repeated campaigns with overwhelming support from this region, which was overwhelmingly Democratic at the time. When World War II ended and nations began striving to conclude agreements to end war and protect human rights, Eleanor Roosevelt played a key role in representing our nation in the formulation of the Universal Declaration of Human Rights. This remarkable document, which could not be formulated and approved in our much more polarized world, has remained the solid foundation and inspiration for generations of individuals and organizations that strive to protect women and girls from abuse.

President Lyndon Johnson used his exceptional influence in the U.S. Congress to orchestrate the passage of civil rights legislation in the mid-1960s, and his wife, Lady Bird, helped in this effort, also exerting her charm and status as first lady to originate the concept of using native shrubs and flowers to beautify highways and cities throughout America. She broke precedent and worked directly with Congress to help pass the Highway Beautification Act and later, in retirement, continued to manage the family's large media conglomerate that she founded before her husband became prominent in politics. Rosalynn and I visited her and her family often during those days.

We first knew Betty Ford when, as first lady, she visited us in the Georgia governor's mansion. In addition to being a stalwart supporter of her husband, President Gerald Ford, she was a pioneer in espousing women's rights. She became famous for her unprecedented support for the Equal Rights Amendment to the U.S. Constitution and for being remarkably outspoken regarding her breast cancer and addiction to drugs when she underwent a mastectomy and later became addicted to painkillers and alcohol. Later she and Rosalynn would go to Washington to lobby for their special projects, approaching both Democratic and Republican legislators to promote legislation to support the treatment of alcoholism, drug addiction, and mental illness.

Not only did my wife play a vital and unprecedented role in my campaigns for governor and president, but she was active in promoting her own projects. She inspired and directed the work of blue-ribbon commissions to promote mental health at the state and federal level and has become a world leader in pursuing this goal since we left the White House. She worked tirelessly, but unsuccessfully, to secure passage of the Equal Rights Amendment, calling hundreds of state legislators to induce them to vote for it. With the exception of state secrets that involved security, I discussed all my major challenges with Rosalynn and sought her advice when I had difficult decisions to make. I did not always accept her recommendations, but my personal staff and cabinet officers knew that their best access to me was through Rosalynn, and she and I shared this knowledge as a personal joke.

Rosalynn has been a full partner with me in founding and operating The Carter Center and, aided by a worldwide group of queens and first ladies, has become the foremost champion of mental health. The Rosalynn Carter Institute for Caregiving does exploratory work on the potential and needs of those who are caring for loved ones suffering from Alzheimer's or other debilitating ailments; tens of thousands of these dedicated volunteers are being trained by a cyber university that telecasts lessons from South Korea. She urged me to write this book and will join me in striving to reach its expressed goals. I hope that all first ladies and other women who occupy positions of influence will adopt this project and pursue it with determination.

The international community has made significant strides in assessing the problems and prescribing cures in the arena of sex discrimination, and official statements, declarations, and covenants have had a beneficial impact. A major international conference on women was held in Copenhagen, Denmark, when I was president. Just its convening in July 1980 was controversial. Our country had been struggling with the failed adoption of the Equal Rights Amendment to the U.S. Constitution, and many countries had reacted adversely to the innovative recommendations issued by the first women's conference five years earlier, in Mexico City. The delegates had set minimum targets for the UN and every nation to meet by 1980, focusing on equal access for women to education, employment, political participation, health services, housing, nutrition, and family planning. Some religious leaders of all faiths openly opposed the idea of sexual equality, as did entrenched politicians who didn't want female challengers and employers who wanted to continue paying less to clothing workers and other female employees. Several of my closest political allies warned me that my endorsement of the meeting would be damaging during the coming presidential election, following my bitter primary battle with Senator Ted Kennedy.

Despite these concerns, there was a consensus that significant progress was being made on women's rights as representatives of 145 nations met in Copenhagen, because the UN General Assembly had recently adopted the Convention on the Elimination of All Forms of Discrimination Against Women (CEDAW), one of the most powerful instruments for women's equality. The Convention, which has been termed "the bill of rights for women," obligates signatory states to report within one year of ratification, and then every four years, on the steps they are taking to comply. It was at this conference that I directed my representative, Sarah Weddington, to sign CEDAW on behalf of the United States.

For Muslims, the Revelation was made by God to protect
the rights of all people, especially those most vulnerable,
and to promote the human dignity of all people. Because of

this, no religious leader can remain silent or refuse to become engaged given the serious discrimination and abuse of many women and young girls in the world today. Any attempt to provide religious justification for refusing girls their right to education or for condoning practices such as female genital cutting, child marriage, exploitation, or enslavement [is] a betrayal of the very principles that religious leaders have the role to defend.

SHEIKH MUHAMED CHÉRIF DIOUP,

ISLAMIC RIGHTS SPECIALIST AND

CHILD PROTECTION OFFICER, TOSTAN, SENEGAL

There was concentrated opposition to the planned participation at the Copenhagen conference of Jehan Sadat, wife of the Egyptian leader who had signed a peace treaty with Israel and was condemned by almost all other members of the Arab League. Unlike other wives of Islamic political leaders, she openly espoused justice for women and had played a key role in promoting a series of legislative reforms in Egypt, known as "Jehan's laws," that greatly enhanced gender equality, such as the right to alimony and custody of children in case of divorce. She is the founder of the Arab-African Women's League and has led unprecedented efforts to promote children's welfare and to endorse peace efforts as an alternative to war in Africa and on other continents. She became world famous as she participated in conferences in many countries, and her condemnation by Arab political and religious leaders has only enhanced her reputation as a spokesperson for women and for peace. Her status as first lady of Egypt changed the global image of Arab women.

I was concerned when many Arab governments ordered their representatives to boycott any speech made by Jehan, because it would be difficult for women from Saudi Arabia, Oman, or the United Arab Emirates to disobey such directives. When her scheduled address approached, those women obeyed their orders to leave the assembly hall, though all of them shook hands with or embraced Jehan on the way out.

The conference closed with a call for all people to:

Involve more men in improving women's roles in society.

Let women exert more political will.

Recognize crucial contributions women were already making to society.

Permit women to participate in planning for the future in all aspects of life.

Assess societal damage caused by a shortage of women in decision-making positions.

Publicize the benefits of women's leadership in cooperatives, day care centers, and credit facilities.

Acknowledge the value of making even small financial resources available to women.

Give women more access to information about their government and untapped opportunities available to them.

The participants also reemphasized the beneficial contributions women could make in promoting peace, enhancing economic progress, ending colonialism and racism, and improving education and health care.

The Convention on the Elimination of All Forms of Discrimination Against Women has now been ratified by all nations except Iran, Palau, Somalia, Sudan, Tonga, and the United States. Its key provision is to prevent "any distinction, exclusion or restriction made on the basis of sex which has the effect or purpose of impairing or nullifying the recognition, enjoyment or exercise by women, irrespective of their marital status, on a basis of equality of men and women, of human rights and fundamental freedoms in the political, economic, social, cultural, civil or any other field." Subsequently two other resolutions of the UN Security Council were adopted, without objection by the United States, and are therefore binding on our country. Resolution 1325 is an international law that requires UN member states to engage women on all levels of decision making on peace and security issues. Resolution 1820 officially links sexual violence as a tactic of war with the maintenance of international peace and security. It also requires that the UN secretary-general make an official report on its implementation and how additional steps can be taken to end sexual violence. Although the scope of CEDAW is much broader than the others, it is obvious that all three international mandates need to be implemented together, as they share a common acknowledgment of the benefits to all people of giving equal status to women and the commitment to strive for this goal.

The issue of abortion is the major impediment to American approval of CEDAW and similar international agreements that protect women's rights. If there is any possibility of encouraging sex education that might lead to the use of contraception or abortion, then Christian fundamentalists, the U.S. Conference of Catholic Bishops, and fervent pro-life activists often join forces and can prevent the passage of otherwise acceptable legislation. There is a consensus within our Christian churches, liberal and conservative, that a developing fetus should be protected whenever possible. This is a difficult issue for me. In many ways, every abortion is an unplanned tragedy, brought about by a combination of human errors, and my Christian faith convinces me that a prospective parent should not make this decision unless the life of the mother is threatened or the pregnancy is caused by rape or incest. I accepted my obligation as president to enforce the Supreme Court ruling in *Roe v. Wade* that authorized some abortions, but I attempted to minimize their number through sex education, making contraceptives more available, special economic assistance for women and infant children, and the promotion of foster parenthood.

Many fervent pro-life activists do not extend their concern to the baby after it is born, ignoring the fact that two-thirds of women who interrupt their pregnancy assert that their primary reason is inability to pay the costs of raising the child. It has long been known that there are fewer abortions in nations where women have access to contraceptives, the assurance that they and their babies will have good health care, and at least enough income to meet their basic needs. And it has been proven that strict prohibitive laws have no significant effect on the number of abortions. The *Lancet* medical journal reported in 2012 that the rate of abortions per 1,000 pregnancies varies from 12 in Western Europe to 23 in the United States and 43 in Eastern Europe. The number exceeds 50 in some nations where there is abject poverty and the use of contraceptives (and abortion) is prohibited.

Good education for women is a positive factor in any society. One of the well-meaning but counterproductive approaches to prevent abortion is to refrain from teaching young Americans how to avoid pregnancy, instruction that is given in many other nations. There is now adequate government funding for sex education, but unfortunately it is quite often tied to a legal prohibition against any mention of contraception, despite the fact that a strong majority of American teenagers report having sex before they are eighteen years old. The Associated Press reported in December 2010 that young people in Western Europe had equal levels of sexual activity, are about equally promiscuous, but, deprived of proper sex education, American girls are much more likely to become pregnant than girls in Western Europe. There were 33 births per 1,000 teenage girls in the United States in 2011, while in Italy the rate was 8, France 7, Germany 5, and in Switzerland 2.

Regardless of how one feels about abortion, there is an inescapable fact in American politics: in order to secure U.S. congressional approval of CEDAW and other international agreements that guarantee women's rights, a provision to preclude promotion or financing of abortions must be accepted. This does not include the prohibition of sex education or the use of contraceptives.

I made one of the major speeches at the historic World Conference on Human Rights in Vienna in 1993, where sexual abuse was discussed at length, and was gratified when, a year later, the Violence Against Women Act (VAWA) was adopted with bipartisan support in the U.S. Congress. The new law recognized that this was a basic premise of the Universal Declaration of Human Rights and would encourage further economic and social progress by bringing more capable women into the mainstream of society. Unfortunately, although VAWA was reauthorized several times, it was allowed to expire in 2012 because of conservative opposition to amendments designed to extend protection to same-sex couples and undocumented immigrants.

Phyllis Schlafly and other women leaders and a number of devout Catholics and Mormons who had opposed the Equal Rights Amendment to the U.S. Constitution were in the forefront of opposition to VAWA, denouncing the legislation as "creating an ideology that all men are guilty and all women are victims" and claiming it was "designed to promote divorce, breakup of marriage and hatred of men." The U.S. Conference of Catholic Bishops opposed the act because it addressed sexual orientation and gender identity. However, with aroused support from other women's organizations and human rights organizations, an expanded bill finally passed both houses of Congress by a 2:1 majority and was signed into law in March 2013.

The language of the new law provides only a partial victory. The international version of this legislation includes required action by nations and international organizations that will put additional economic and political pressure on countries known to be especially abusive to women, but this provision has not yet been adopted by the United States. The much more incisive international version of the bill has been introduced in the U.S. House of Representatives by a bipartisan group of members of Congress, and there are indications of similar support from both parties in the Senate. Its primary sponsor, Representative Jan Schakowsky, Democrat of Illinois, says:

> Violence against women is a humanitarian tragedy, a vicious crime, a global health catastrophe, a roadblock to social and

economic development and a threat to national security. . . .
Sexual violence has been systematically used to destroy communities and to instill a sense of despair and hopelessness
within a population. IVAWA would make ending violence
against women a U.S. foreign policy priority, promote health
programs and survivor services, civil and criminal legal pro-
tections, educational opportunities and economic opportunities for women and girls. Passage of IVAWA would give
us critical tools in the fight against gender-based violence
around the world.

This is an impasse that needs to be resolved, which could make the
United States the preeminent driving force in reducing sexual violence
of all kinds.

For many centuries there has been a debate about the best way to
reduce the extent of prostitution and the forced female slavery and
spread of sexually transmitted diseases it precipitates. During the past
few years I have spoken with the ministers of health in two European
countries that have taken opposite approaches. One of these approaches
seems to be having a beneficial effect.

The Dutch government decided in 2000 that the best way to control prostitution, reduce the rate of sexually transmitted diseases, and
protect women and girls from abuse was to legalize prostitution and the
operation of brothels while regulating the trade. I remember how surprised I was to walk down the street on my first visit to Amsterdam and
pass windows in which attractive women were displaying themselves.
The intent of the law was to give the prostitutes some protection by is-
suing work permits and mandatory health inspections. A sex tourism
boom resulted, and in 2008 there were 142 licensed brothels in Amsterdam and about five hundred window displays. However, a former
mayor of the city has stated that the enormous business of more than

$100 million annually has been largely taken over by Eastern European crime syndicates that are trafficking women and illegal drugs. So, although prostitution remains legal, there is now a government move to rescue these women and help them find other trades.

Sweden tried for a hundred years to pass legislation making illegal the purchase of sex by men, and when new legislation was drafted and debated in 1999 this was the key issue. There was a strong sentiment that the women themselves should not be punished, since it was believed that many were improperly enticed or actually forced into prostitution. Although Sweden has the highest proportion of women parliamentarians in Europe, they were divided on the key issues. The final legislation made it illegal to buy sexual services, to act as a pimp, or to operate a brothel, but the prostitutes were not considered to be acting illegally. The number of sex workers in Sweden dropped more than 40 percent during the next five years, and their prices have also fallen.

Other European countries watched these two experiments closely, and both Norway and Iceland passed laws similar to Sweden's. Nick Kristof reports, "Customers can easily find an underage Eastern European girl working as a prostitute in Amsterdam, but not in Stockholm." Germany adopted the Dutch model in dealing with prostitution and found that the trade increased by 70 percent in its larger cities. As I write this, in December 2013, the most intense public debate in France is whether to adopt a law similar to that in Sweden. The legislation has passed the Assembly and is expected to be approved by the Senate in June 2014. At the same time, the Supreme Court of Canada voted unanimously to strike down the country's three basic laws governing the sex trade: prohibiting the operation of a brothel, banning pimping and preventing prostitutes from hiring security guards, and making soliciting or communicating to clients illegal. The Parliament was given a year to devise alternative legislation.

The key to the relative success of Sweden's approach is to prescribe punishment for those who own and operate the brothels and control the women, as well as the male customers who provide the profit motive.

This was the strong recommendation of participants in our Human Rights Defenders Forum who are trying to control the trafficking of women in Atlanta and other places where sexual slavery is rampant. There is little doubt that public exposure in a trial and the imposition of a heavy fine or jail time for prominent male citizens or police officers who patronize or profit from the sex trade would be extremely effective. The opposite policy still exists in the United States, where there are fifty times as many female prostitutes arrested as their male customers and handlers.

There was one encouraging case in Atlanta in September 2013, when a pimp was sentenced to life imprisonment for abusing a fifteen-year-old girl. He was found guilty by a jury on charges including human trafficking, pimping, aggravated sodomy, child molestation, statutory rape, and false imprisonment. The convicted man had contacted the teenager online before meeting her in person the previous November, imprisoned her in his home, raped her, and then set up appointments for male customers in various hotels and took all the money she collected. This teenager was one of the more fortunate: she was able to obtain a cell phone from one of her customers and called her parents; they notified the police, and she was rescued after a relatively short period in captivity.

Pastor Paul Palmer is the founder of the Atlanta Dream Center, whose mission is to serve and rescue minors held in sexual slavery in that city, and during our conference he was asked what religious leaders could do to address this terrible crime. He responded with some emotion, "Buyers do not wake up and think that they want to go out and buy children. They start with something else, pornography or perhaps they were abused as young boys, and tend to struggle with abusive expressions of masculinity. We have not taught men that we need to honor these women as our sisters. . . . We have failed in religious leadership because we have assumed that this is just what young men are going to go through. We must take a stand and say 'No more!' "

Morocco has provided a sterling example of what can be done to enhance women's rights in a political environment where Islamic law is a powerful factor. The first time we visited the country, more than thirty years ago, Rosalynn and I traveled to Fez, Marrakech, and other cities before returning to Rabat to meet with King Hassan II. He had become a good friend of my mother; he told me they engaged in surprisingly personal banter. As his guest on an earlier visit to Morocco, she had declined a gift of several bottles of expensive perfume, claiming that she had no room in her luggage. He promised to deliver the gift in person, and when he and his two sons came to the White House on a state visit, the king asked that Mama attend the official ceremonies. That first night he knocked on her door and with a broad smile presented her with an enormous bottle of Chanel #5 perfume. She exclaimed, "You're just like every other man off on a trip without his wife!" I doubt that anyone had ever spoken to His Majesty in this way.

We laughed about my mother's comment when we had supper later as the king's guests in the palace and had a delightful conversation about family affairs. He commented that he was trying to find a wife for his oldest son, Mohammed, and explained that it was the custom in Morocco for a prince to marry the daughter of a nonrelated desert chieftain, who was believed to have strains of independence and vigor in her genes. Prospective brides would be presented at the palace and "tried before selection" by the prince. His Majesty complained that Mohammed had decided to do his own choosing. In the end the Crown Prince married Salma Bennani, who is the daughter of a schoolteacher and has a degree in engineering. As Princess Lalla Salma, she is the first wife of a Moroccan king to receive a royal title; others had been known simply as "mother of the king's children" or something equivalent.

King Mohammed VI now rules the kingdom, and, over substantial opposition, including massive public demonstrations, he proposed improvements in the status of Moroccan women. In 2004 the Parliament finally accepted his proposals. The new laws raised the minimum age of marriage to eighteen unless exceptions are made by a judge, prescribed husband and wife equal and with joint responsibility for their family, granted women more rights in setting the terms of marriage contracts, and did away with mandatory male guardians when a girl comes of age. Women can no longer be married against their will, nor are they subservient to their husband in child-rearing decisions, and any marriage disputes must be settled within a month. Whichever parent cares for the children owns the house. Both daughters and sons have the right to inherit property, and children born out of wedlock can acknowledge their own paternity. King Hassan II had two wives, but the new law permits a second marriage only if a judge determines that there are exceptional reasons for it, if the first wife gives her approval, and if the husband proves that he can support two families. A divorce can be granted only in a secular court, with no religious involvement, and attempts at reconciliation must first be exhausted. If spouses have independent incomes, they can negotiate a contract separate from the marriage vows concerning the management and ownership of assets.

Other Islamic kingdoms, and all Western nations, should implement these reforms.

A partnership between a political leader and an actress provides another example of rapid progress in resolving a serious problem. The abuse of women in the Bosnian war was the subject of a dramatic motion picture, *In the Land of Blood and Honey*, produced and directed by Angelina Jolie. British foreign secretary William Hague was encouraged by one of his assistants to watch an advance screening of the film, and it convinced him to launch a major diplomatic effort to publicize the problem of rape in war zones and marshal as much international support as possible for corrective actions by governments. In May 2012 he announced an alliance with Jolie, who was special envoy to the UN High Commissioner for Refugees, pledging to establish a seventy-member team from the United Kingdom that would be deployed to war zones to gather evidence and testimony for use in the prosecution of those involved in sexual violence in conflict zones, to encourage individual nations to adopt more effective laws, and to utilize doctors, lawyers, police, and others to protect and care for rape victims. Secretary Hague and Ms. Jolie declared that more than twenty thousand women were raped in Bosnia and Herzegovina, more than fifty thousand in Sierra Leone, and at least 250,000 were raped during the one hundred days of genocide in Rwanda in 1994. Only a few men have ever been brought to justice for these crimes. Similar reports are now emerging from the civil conflict in Syria.

Hague and Jolie recently visited eastern Congo and Rwanda to meet survivors of sexual abuse and with regional political leaders who claim to have some authority over the militia groups who are known to be the brutal rapists. The foreign secretary pointed out that rape is used as a weapon of war in conflict zones and that, more often than not, the international community ignores these brutal crimes and so the perpetrators repeat the cycle of abuse. It was reported that 74 percent of survivors of rape treated in a hospital in Goma, in eastern Congo, were children, and eleven baby girls between the ages of six and twelve months had been raped! Jolie said, "For too long these innocent victims of war, responsible for none of the harm, have been bearing the worst of the pain."

Three weeks later Hague presided over a meeting of foreign ministers from Canada, France, Germany, Italy, Japan, Russia, and the United States, who all approved a new international agreement declaring that rape and sexual violence are grave violations of the Geneva Conventions and that universal jurisdiction can apply; it also provided for documentation and investigation of these crimes to be used in the prosecution of the guilty. In hopes of preventing such crimes altogether, a primary thrust of the agreement is that perpetrators of sexual violence will not be granted immunity in peace treaties. When the United Kingdom acted as president of the UN Security Council in June 2013, Foreign Secretary Hague used this opportunity to open the debate on sexual violence in conflicts. The result was a unanimous vote for a Security Council resolution on the subject, with forty-five nations as cosponsors. When I visited Secretary Hague in July 2013, he told me that he intended to convene a global gathering on the same subject during the UN General Assembly in September 2013, and he met this commitment. This recent effort by a diplomat and a movie star to force the long-ignored issue of rape during wartime onto the international agenda has been a notable achievement.

One of my personal heroes is Ela Bhatt, also an Elder, from India. Her parents were Brahmins, and she received a superb education leading to a law degree. In 1955 she joined the legal department of the Textile Labor Association (TLA), founded by Mahatma Gandhi, and soon became the leader of its women's wing. In 1972, when the textile mills of Ahmedabad, India's fifth largest city, were failing and workers were laid off, Ela visited their neighborhood and found that the women were supporting their family through vending and home-based work like sewing and cigarette rolling. This work was low-paying and exploitative. She became increasingly concerned when she realized that there were state laws protecting industrial workers but not the thousands of self-employed women who worked to provide their family with an income. She organized them into the Self-Employed Women's Association (SEWA), with herself as the general secretary. She followed the example of Gandhi, who believed that an organization of workers should cover all aspects of their lives as a holistic defense against oppressive laws or state policies. SEWA was soon seen as more militant than the TLA, and the interests of the self-employed women were sometimes at odds with those working in large factories.

There were riots in 1981, when high-caste Indians protested the reservation of jobs and opportunities for untouchables. Since a large portion of SEWA members were from the untouchable caste, Ela and SEWA defended the downtrodden group. They were expelled from the TLA for their outspokenness, but the result was that SEWA expanded rapidly in membership and influence. Today SEWA is the largest primary union in India, with 1.7 million women members. Ela has formed more than a hundred cooperatives among women who were extremely poor; nearly three-fourths lived on less than 20 cents a day and had no prospect of income after their working days were over. Now there are more than 100,000 women enrolled in SEWA's health and life insurance program and 350,000 depositors in its bank. Most loans are in the neighborhood of $100, and even with a fairly high interest rate of about 15 percent to cover administrative costs, the bank reports that the repayment rate exceeds 97 percent.

In accepting the Indira Gandhi Prize for Peace, Disarmament and Development in February 2013, Ela Bhatt described the character and contribution of working women with these beautiful words:

> I have faith in women. . . . In my experience, as I have seen within India and in other countries, women are the key to rebuilding a community. Why? Focus on women and you will find an ally who wants a stable community. She wants roots for her family. You get a worker, a provider, a caretaker, an educator, a networker, a forger of bonds. I consider thousands of poor working women's participation and representation an integral part of the peace and development process. Women bring constructive, creative and sustainable solutions to the table. . . . A woman who tends a small plot of land, grows vegetables, weaves cloth, and provides for the family and the market, while caring for the financial, social, educational and emotional needs of her family is a multifunctional worker and the builder of a stable society.

During deliberations of The Elders, Ela usually listens to our debates without interrupting; then she raises her hand and everyone gets quiet to listen. On almost any issue she can point out how it affects the well-being of poor female workers, and she invariably describes how their proper treatment and incorporation into the larger society can be of benefit to everyone. She defines women's poverty as "violence with social consent."

Violence against women is the most prevalent and the most hidden injustice in our world today. As I lay out in my book *On God's Side*, what has been missing from this narrative is the condemnation of these behaviors from other men, especially men in positions of power, authority, and influence— like those in our pulpits. In a section of that book, I say "we need to establish a firm principle: the abuse of women by men will no longer be tolerated by other men." The voices of more men need to join the chorus to make that perfectly clear.

JIM WALLIS, AUTHOR, FOUNDER AND EDITOR OF
Sojourners MAGAZINE

After years of concerted effort by The Carter Center to alleviate the mistreatment of women and girls, one of the most important lessons we have learned is that outside organizations like ours, even when working with women who are fighting their own abuse, cannot bring about an end to child marriage, genital cutting, or exclusion of women from equal treatment without the support of the entire community, especially including traditional chiefs and other male leaders. Molly Melching, the head of Tostan, said that when men were asked to join their discussion groups the women began calling their goal "human rights" instead of "women's rights." Including men had a positive effect, because Tostan began making real progress in ending genital cutting and child marriage only when the men gave their quiet approval or began speaking out in favor of the reforms. One of the most effective inducements for local chiefs and other men to oppose child marriage, for instance, is to show them how families can become more prosperous if the girls can go to school and be gainfully employed rather than sold at an early age to become a servant in their husband's home.

After attending one of our local human rights sessions in the Democratic Republic of Congo, a traditional chief attended our Human Rights Defenders Forum in Atlanta and then returned home to discover that a local soldier had raped a fourteen-year-old girl. The chief personally found the soldier, tied him to a chair, and waited for the police to arrive and arrest him. He then used his influence to prevent anyone from condemning or ostracizing the girl. The benefits from this kind of bold action have been proven in Malawi, Senegal, Liberia, Ghana, and other African countries. When some of these leaders have recognized the societal advantages of making changes, they have become effective spokesmen among their own people and in nationwide councils.

Another good example comes from the *Atlantic* magazine, which in June 2013 told the story of an English teacher named Kwataine in central Malawi. As a young man he had seen a woman struggling in labor; unable to reach the local health clinic in time to stop her bleeding, she died. When Kwataine became chief, he decided that all women should have a "secret mother" to advise her during pregnancy and then should be attended by a qualified person at the time of birth. He imposed fines of a goat or a chicken if the family permitted a woman to go into labor in her home without care. His strict policies have resulted in no maternal deaths during the past three years, whereas there were forty in his district in 2007. Kwataine is now recruiting young girls as skilled midwives and has set a goal of having two thousand midwives by 2015. The president of Malawi, Joyce Banda, has recognized his good work and is offering Kwataine as an example for the other twenty thousand chiefs in the country.

What prevents us from following the example of Kwataine and the Congo chief and taking action to secure basic human rights for women? Some of us are paralyzed by the extent and complexity of the problems. Some of us have become desensitized by societal violence and no longer recognize it when it occurs. Some have misinterpreted Holy Scripture and believe God has ordained a lower status for women. Some men are afraid of losing their advantages in a paternalistic society. But these two simple success stories illustrate how the suffering of women and girls can be alleviated by an individual's forceful action and how the benefits of such actions stretch out into the larger society. Political and religious leaders share a special responsibility, but the fact is that all of us can act within our own spheres of influence to meet the challenges.

My hope is that this book and the publicity that will result from its promotion will be of help. The Elders will continue to devote significant effort to fighting discrimination and abuse of women and girls, and all of us at The Carter Center are eager to contribute whatever resources we have to join others in this effort. For example, The Center's initiative Mobilizing Faith for Women is preparing to offer an online resource for those who wish to be involved, either by being inspired to take action or by reporting on what they are doing. The following are actions that we will monitor and support, and we encourage readers to visit our website, www.cartercenter.org, and participate with us in this effort.

1. Encourage women and girls, including those not abused, to speak out more forcefully. It is imperative that those who do speak out are protected from retaliation.
2. Remind political and religious leaders of the abuses and what they can do to alleviate them.
3. Encourage these same leaders to become supporters of the United Nations High Commissioner for Human Rights and other UN agencies that advance human rights and peace.
4. Encourage religious and political leaders to relegate warfare and violence to a last resort as a solution to terrorism and national security challenges.
5. Abandon the death penalty and seek to rehabilitate criminals instead of relying on excessive incarceration, especially for non-violent offenders.

6. Marshal the efforts of women officeholders and first ladies, and encourage involvement of prominent civilian women in correcting abuses.

7. Induce individual nations to elevate the end of human trafficking to a top priority, as they did to end slavery in the nineteenth century.

8. Help remove commanding officers from control over cases of sexual abuse in the military so that professional prosecutors can take action.

9. Apply Title IX protection for women students and evolve laws and procedures in all nations to reduce the plague of sexual abuse on university campuses.

10. Include women's rights specifically in new UN Millennium Development Goals.

11. Expose and condemn infanticide of baby girls and selective abortion of female fetuses.

12. Explore alternatives to battered women's shelters, such as installing GPS locators on male abusers, and make police reports of spousal abuse mandatory.

13. Strengthen UN and other legal impediments to ending genital mutilation, child marriage, trafficking, and other abuses of girls and women.

14. Increase training of midwives and other health workers to provide care at birth.

15. Help scholars working to clarify religious beliefs on protecting women's rights and nonviolence, and give activists and practitioners access to such training resources.

16. Insist that the U.S. Senate ratify the Convention on the Elimination of All Forms of Discrimination Against Women.

17. Insist that the United States adopt the International Violence Against Women Act.

18. Encourage more qualified women to seek public office, and support them.

19. Recruit influential men to assist in gaining equal rights for women.

20. Adopt the Swedish model by prosecuting pimps, brothel owners, and male customers, not the prostitutes.

21. Publicize and implement UN Security Resolution 1325, which encourages the participation of women in peace efforts.

22. Publicize and implement UN Security Resolution 1820, which condemns the use of sexual violence as a tool of war.

23. Condemn and outlaw honor killings.

ACKNOWLEDGMENTS

I want to express special thanks to Karin Ryan and my other partners at The Carter Center who made it possible for me to write this book. As our leading specialist on human rights, Karin has orchestrated our annual assembly of human rights heroes from around the world, which we call Human Rights Defenders Forums. Over the years, she has emphasized the increasing importance of discrimination against women as an issue for us to address, and has assembled the foremost protectors of women's rights to share their information and advice with us. The incisive comments of some of the key participants in our 2013 session were especially useful to me.

This is the eleventh time that I have enjoyed the benefit of having Alice Mayhew as editor, and she and the other editors and designers at Simon & Schuster have been of great help. Their generous stream of questions, suggestions, and corrections have made the entire process both challenging and gratifying.

Since 1981, Dr. Steve Hochman has monitored my university lectures, my speeches, and the texts of all my books, and his emphasis on clarity and accuracy continues to increase my own desire to reach his high standards.

INDEX

ABOUT THE AUTHOR

Jimmy Carter was the 39th President of the United States, serving from 1977 to 1981. In 1982, he and his wife founded The Carter Center, a nonprofit organization dedicated to improving the lives of people around the world. Carter was awarded the Nobel Peace Prize in 2002. He is the author of more than two dozen books, including *An Hour Before Daylight*, *Palestine Peace Not Apartheid*, and *Our Endangered Values*. He lives in Plains, Georgia.